9.14

Teaching the Cello
to Groups

JEAN HORSFALL

LONDON
OXFORD UNIVERSITY PRESS
NEW YORK   TORONTO
1974

Oxford University Press, Ely House, London W.1

GLASGOW   NEW YORK   TORONTO   MELBOURNE   WELLINGTON
CAPE TOWN   IBADAN   NAIROBI   DAR ES SALAAM   LUSAKA   ADDIS ABABA
DELHI   BOMBAY   CALCUTTA   MADRAS   KARACHI   LAHORE   DACCA
KUALA LUMPUR   SINGAPORE   HONG KONG   TOKYO

ISBN 0 19 315510 5
© Oxford University Press 1974

787.3
1817

PRINTED IN GREAT BRITAIN
BY EBENEZER BAYLIS AND SON, LTD.
THE TRINITY PRESS, WORCESTER, AND LONDON

Contents

Introduction   1

1   Equipment and Teaching Space   7
2   Starting the Group   17
3   Planning the Work   26
4   The Stages in Detail—Stage I   33
5   The Stages in Detail—Stages II and III   53
6   Backward and Forward Extensions   60
7   Fourth Position, Half Position, Vibrato,
        and Harmonics   67
8   Third and Second Positions; The Tenor Clef   79
9   The Elementary Cellist in the Orchestra   87
10 Incentives   94

Conclusion   101
Appendix I—Notes on Scale Fingerings and
    Thumb Positions   103
Appendix II—Teaching Material   107

55859

Introduction

In all teaching there is a constant challenge to keep up with (or better still, ahead of) new ideas in education, new attitudes among the children, and indeed new concepts on the part of the parents. As I believe that flexibility and change are the basis of all the best teaching it is with some hesitation that I have agreed to put into print my ideas on cello group teaching.

This book, therefore, is offered as a guide and possible framework for others embarking on the same work. I hope that they in their turn will build on it and search constantly for better ways of doing things, other ways of stimulating pupils' imagination and interest, new approaches and techniques.

There are many schools of cello playing, many differing ideas about holding the bow, left-hand techniques and fingerings, even playing position. Obviously I teach the kind of technique I find satisfactory and, therefore, my suggestions about bow-hold drills relate to that technique, but I hope that teachers with other ideas will be able to separate the group teaching technique from the playing technique and adapt their method of approach accordingly.

At the same time, perhaps, the outlines given in this book will save a few heart-searchings and a great deal of wear and tear for those who have very little experience of instrumental class work, particularly with cellists.

Many people still question whether group teaching of stringed instruments is either practical or desirable. Quite apart from economic factors I am convinced that it is both, provided that the teaching is well done and that a proper group technique is used, and provided also that children can be moved from group to group according to progress and that, as they become sufficiently advanced, individual lessons are available. The difficulties of securing good intonation with a class of five or six doing a great deal of position work are so frustrating to teacher and pupil alike as to be almost worse than useless.

In the elementary stages pupils learn from each other, they learn to play with each other, and a carefully fostered spirit of emulation in the group will work wonders in stimulating practice. They also find that others have similar difficulties and this is a great help when the going becomes hard. Some problems affect the cello group more than others. Quite apart from the fact that children will develop and progress at different speeds (I have tried to offer some suggestions for dealing with this in the course of the later chapters in this book), there are the physical difficulties of space, accommodation, instruments, and manipulation which all cellists, but few players of other instruments, appreciate. The instrument is large, fragile, rarely has a case that gives any protection at all against knocks, and contains one essential part (the end-pin) which tends to fall out or slip in at the wrong moments, and which, when adjusted for playing, is a perfect obstacle for everyone to fall over unless the greatest possible care is taken. The playing position can be acutely uncomfortable unless the chairs are the right shape and there is enough room. These and other difficulties confront the would-be cellist at every session.

The teacher is most likely to be a visitor to the school and may only come once a week, possibly in the lunch hour or after 4 o'clock. In these circumstances liaison with the full-time staff at the school is exceedingly difficult, but if group teaching is to succeed it is essential, and some way must be found to make and maintain contact. Many schools appoint a 'liaison officer', usually the head of music or a music specialist, but in smaller schools sometimes an interested member of staff or even the head (though that overworked individual rarely has the time). This usually ensures smooth working, although even then it is very necessary that the peripatetic teacher should make a habit of visiting the staff room, meeting as many members of staff as possible, and making himself known and liked, or at least understood.

Frequent study of the notice board in the staff room is also necessary; it is too easy for the liaison officer to forget to tell the visiting teacher that lessons must be cancelled next week because of examinations, sports days, speech days, etc. The children rarely remember.

Staff-room gossip will frequently throw light on the problems of a difficult child, and conversely the experience of a visiting teacher with certain members of his group may have something to offer the class-, year-, or house-teacher concerned. It is vital to know whether a child has a real excuse for missing a lesson, whether he has a history of sickness or bad eyesight or difficulties at home. A good visiting teacher will never accept a verbal message sent via another child in the group without checking with a member of staff who is likely to know the real reason for absence.

Many of these difficulties will vanish automatically if the teacher is a full-time member of the school staff, but in the nature of things this will rarely happen.

One more point should be made. It happens frequently that a violinist is asked to take a cello group, on the assumption that the instruments, belonging as they do to the same family, are played in the same way. This is not so; they are *quite different*. If a violinist is in this position then he or she must have lessons from a good cellist who can pinpoint the differences in technique quite clearly. The cellist who is asked to teach violinists is likely to be in equal difficulties and should take violin lessons from a colleague as a matter of urgency. Otherwise the results are apt to be disastrous. Another thoroughly bad practice is to ask a teacher to take violins, violas, cellos, and even basses together in one orchestral group, on the principle that because it is done with brass instruments it can be done with strings. This is not really so, and any teacher put in this position should fight to have it altered. It is frustrating and time-wasting for all concerned, the results are usually poor, and a shorter time given to the instruments separately would always be better.

This does not mean that there should not be an orchestra. Children should be admitted to an orchestra playing music suitable to their standard as soon as possible, but this is by way of revision of their group lessons and a social outlet, not for teaching technique.

Finally, I would summarize the basic requirements for a really successful cello group teacher as follows:

(i) An orderly idea of what is to be taught over each year.
(ii) A plan for every lesson, prepared beforehand and written down.
(iii) The ability to demonstrate the points to be taught and to say as little as possible.
(iv) Punctuality.
(v) Reasonably good physical conditions in which to teach (see Chapter 1).
(vi) A sense of humour.

(vii) Ability to co-operate with, and understand the difficulties of, schools that are visited.

A car, the constitution of an ox, and endless patience will also help!

1 Equipment and Teaching Space

To operate a cello group successfully the following are essential:

(i)   Enough space.
(ii) Suitable chairs.
(iii) Suitable well-fitted instruments.
(iv) Adequate storage space in school.

It is also desirable, but not essential, to have—

(i)   End-pin holders.
(ii) Access to a piano.
(iii) A chalk board.
(iv) Somewhere where charts may be displayed.
(v)   (at a later date) Proper music stands as opposed to music desks with tilting tops, which are rarely satisfactory for cellists.

Spare strings and equipment to deal with very minor repairs must also be available, either in school or from the teacher.

I. THE SIZE OF THE TEACHING ROOM

It is desirable to allow a square of 132 cm. by 132 cm. for every cellist except the smallest children, this measurement to include the chair the pupil sits on. It must be possible to use the full length of the bow on all strings and to move it freely without fear of colliding with the next-door player, a stand, a desk, or anything else in the room. There must be space for the teacher to move around and it should be possible for every member of the group to see charts or the blackboard, if this is being used.

So a fairly large room is needed. A small school hall is ideal, but rarely available and often too noisy. If a classroom is used it must be possible to move the desks or tables in such a way that enough clear space is left for mobility. A classroom of 55 sq.m. with twenty-five desks in it will necessitate a lot of furniture removing before six cellists can be accommodated. On the other hand, I have taught three cellists in a small room 3 m. by 5 m. by having them in a half-circle. But this is *not* to be recommended. The teacher must consider all the factors and discuss them with the school concerned. Sometimes it is difficult for the school to make a suitable room available and a compromise has to be made. I have taught in some excellent cloakrooms which fulfilled my needs very well! On the other hand, a teacher saddled with an impossible room should lose no chance of demonstrating the difficulties he is working under, which are not always appreciated by other members of staff.

2. SUITABLE CHAIRS

This is a point of fundamental importance to all cellists. Chairs should have straight seats and be of the right height for the players. The following chairs should be avoided at all costs:

(i)   Tubular stacking chairs with canvas seats.
(ii) Any chairs with seats curving up in front.
(iii) Any wooden stacking chairs with seats curving up at the sides.

If nothing else is available but this type of chair then use must be made of books, coats, cushions, or even canvas

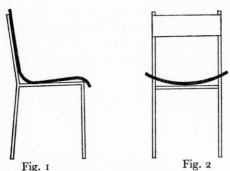

Fig. 1   Fig. 2
Unsuitable types of chair

cello-cases to make the seat as flat as possible. If this is not done bad posture and/or cramp will certainly ensue.

The height of the chair is also very important. As a rough guide I think of a cello player working in a series of right angles. The angle at hips and at the knees should be as near 90° as possible. This can only be achieved if the chair is the right height for the player, and if the player sits on the front half of the seat. Figs. 3 and 4, and Plates 1 and 2 illustrate the point:

Fig. 3   Fig. 4
Diagrams to show the bad leg positions dictated by a chair which is too high (Fig. 3) or too low (Fig. 4)

(N.B. These remarks apply to the conventional type of end-pin usually found on school cellos. The bent end-pin demands a different playing position and those using it would be able to adjust their demands accordingly. A straight-seated chair is still vital.)

3. THE INSTRUMENT, BOW, AND CASE

Well-fitted instruments of the right size are essential to the success of the group. Instruments are available in $\frac{1}{4}$, $\frac{1}{2}$, $\frac{3}{4}$, and full-sizes, although the smaller ones are frequently difficult to get. The advent of Suzuki methods means that $\frac{1}{8}$th and $\frac{1}{16}$th size cellos will also be available soon. It is, however, disastrous to start a child on a cello which is too big. The strain on back, shoulders, and hands is very great, and bad posture or frustration usually result; sometimes, even, there can be more serious physical damage. If the cello is not much too large, adaptations with height of chair and length of end-pin can be made, and in this way a child with a large hand can often manage a bigger cello than his height suggests. Length of back and legs must also be borne in mind and (with older girls particularly) vital statistics. A girl who is well developed round the bust may have real difficulty in fitting herself behind the instrument! In this case it is well worth trying several so-called full-size cellos. The back lengths of the instruments vary considerably, and it is not always the longer back that is the greatest help in this kind of difficulty.

Unfortunately, there is no quick rule of thumb by which a teacher may judge the correct size of cello. There are too many variables. I have taught a child of $10\frac{1}{2}$ on a full-size cello and one of 13 who found a $\frac{3}{4}$ size instrument a strain. One can only look and try to see that the C peg is just clear of the shoulder, that the knees are on or near the lower bouts, and that the instrument is held comfortably against the chest at about an angle of 45°–50°.

Before the lessons start the teacher should, if possible, check every instrument. Regrettably, at the moment of writing, many new cellos are being sent out by manufacturers in an unplayable condition. Every full-size cello should have a sharp-pointed end-pin which has an overall length of at least 35 cm. Under no circumstances should this length be less, and any cello arriving with a shorter one should be returned immediately to have a new end-pin fitted. Bridges should show no signs of warping, should be well shaped at the top, and should have feet which fit flush with the belly of the instrument at all points. The height of the bridge should be governed by the type of strings with which the instrument is fitted. Metal strings demand less clearance of the fingerboard than gut. Pegs should fit properly on both sides of the scroll and have a well-drilled hole for the strings, and if metal strings are used adjusters *must be fitted*.

Too many Education Authorities, in a misguided effort to cut costs, accept and issue cellos with metal strings and no adjusters. These instruments are more trouble than they are worth, and the cost of correct fitting initially is relatively so small that teachers should, in their own interest and that of the children, press for correct fitting. If an older cello, which has previously been fitted with gut strings, is to be converted to metal strings, it should be sent to a qualified instrument repairer, as the bass bar inside the instrument will probably need strengthening and the bridge must be adapted too.

In all this, reference may be made to the British Standards pamphlet No. 3499, Part 5, 1964 'Recommendations to

Purchasers of stringed instruments' which sets out basic guidelines and is a great source of help and information.

The bow should also be scrutinized carefully. The screw should work easily (often a child's hands are not very strong) and should produce the correct tension without difficulty. If it fails to do this, the bow should be returned as the hair is probably too long or the screw faulty. At tension the stick should curve inwards slightly, but deviate neither to right nor left at the point. Older bows should have an adequate amount of hair which is reasonably clean. If a bow is very greasy, but does not seem to need a re-hair, washing is a simple matter for horsehair (see end of chapter). New bows rarely come with resin on and, ideally, these (and newly washed bows) should be treated with powdered resin before block resin is applied. Every child should be encouraged to buy resin (if some is not supplied with the outfit) and then use it frequently.

Cases are very important. They should be of good strong waterproof canvas or similar material with a reinforced carrying handle. Children should be taught to use the case whenever the cello is to be taken out of doors, and actively discouraged from taking it into the open air 'undressed', even if the distance is a short walk between two blocks of school buildings, or it is going home in a car. Very occasionally a block some distance away from the concert hall is used as a green room for school concerts: in this case, cellos may have to be taken across without covers, but the iniquities of the situation should be made quite clear to the organizer concerned.

Storage of cellos in school. This presents considerable difficulties. If possible (and if space is available), a special rack should be built in a store-room which can be locked and which is near, or even leads off, the music room. This

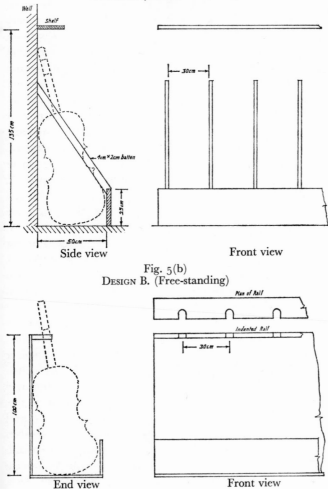

Fig. 5(a)
Racks for cellos
DESIGN A (attached to a wall)

Side view

Front view

Fig. 5(b)
DESIGN B. (Free-standing)

End view

Front view

store-room should not contain a heater or heating pipes, and should be dry and of an even temperature. The racks themselves, which can also be placed in the music rooms, can be very simple (see Figs. 5a and 5b). Suggestions may be found in H.M.S.O. Building Bulletin 'Music and Drama in Schools', and I have also found the two designs on p. 13 effective: the first will take cellos in cases, the second is really better for instruments without cases.

Wooden storage cases are cumbersome, attract wood-worm, and take up too much room. If racks cannot be built then use should be made of the tops of cupboards and odd corners, bearing in mind that the cellos *must* be kept as far away as possible from the heating system, and never allowed to touch heating pipes. If corners are used cellos should be placed bridge inwards, and corners behind inward opening doors should be avoided unless it is quite impossible for the door to be flung back and damage the instrument.

End-pin holders. To protect the floors and to prevent much trouble with end-pins slipping on polished wood-blocks, tiles, etc., simple end-pin holders are desirable. The most portable is a broad strap or strong belt, one end of which can be placed under a front leg of the player's chair so that the end-pin can be placed in one of the eyelets. If a loose-textured mat is available this will prove satisfactory, provided it is long enough for one end to be secured under the player's chair leaving plenty of room (about 70 cm.) projecting for the reception of the end-pin. A slip mat will not do.

The best gadgets for school, because they are solid and can be made quite easily in the woodwork room, are wooden end-pin rests. These can be T-shaped (Fig. 6a) or just a flat bar of wood (Fig. 6b) which has either a hole drilled for the chair leg at one end or a short strap attached to form a loop round the chair leg. With the T-shaped gadget the cross-bar will fit behind the legs of the chair and the tail section will have indentations drilled in it (about 5 mm. deep to take the spike (see diagrams). Neither of these is very effective with tubular stacking chairs although the T-shaped one can be made to do.

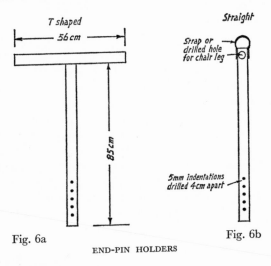

Fig. 6a   Fig. 6b

END-PIN HOLDERS

Various commercial gadgets are also available, some more successful than others.

Finally, there is the matter of the equipment the teacher himself should carry around. It is desirable, but not essential, that he should take his own instrument: provided a spare one is available in the school for demonstration to the group he may be able to leave his own cello at home, and I know successful teachers who rely on 'local' cellos in all their teaching. Spare strings, resin, tweezers to help in threading strings through pegholes, pliers which will fit both pegs, end-pins, and end-pin screws, and something to ease recalcitrant pegs should all be in his case. Spare tailgut and bridges may be useful, but unless the teacher is a handyman, and has time available, the fitting of both on cellos is such an important and vital job that it is best done by an expert well away from the pressure of the classroom. Sandpaper may be useful, and those who are expert with a soundpost setter will not want to be without one.

Add to this list charts (of which more later) and music, notebook, and register, and it will be seen that a car is highly desirable if not a virtual necessity. It is often hard to convince an authority, especially an urban one, that a car is needed. I have found, over the years, that the increased efficiency and improved health which comes from having one (not to mention the fact that an authority can frequently have the odd instrument transported for it by the teacher) more than offset the extra cost of a travel allowance from the employer's point of view. Even if no travel allowance is forthcoming, the comfort and convenience will make a car for this work a valuable investment for the teacher.

Note: HOW TO WASH BOWS

(i) Add a tablespoon of household ammonia to a pint of very hot water in a bowl.

(ii) Remove the screw from the bow.

(iii Swish the hair in the water taking care *never* (a) to twist the hair or (b) to get any other part of the bow wet.

(iv) Put a drop of light oil on the screw and replace, making sure the hair is not twisted, and having dabbed surplus water from the hair with a towel.

(v) Hang up to dry.

2 Starting the Group

I. THE SIZE OF THE GROUP

Many factors will govern the size of the cello group. Regional Local Authority regulations must be taken into consideration. There must be enough instruments available (sharing is possible for a short time, but soon becomes frustrating in the extreme). It may even be difficult to find enough starters. In any case, as will be seen from the last chapter, there must be enough space in which to teach adequately.

I have found four to six pupils a comfortable number to teach in the elementary stages. If there are fewer it is tempting to give short individual lessons rather than to treat them as a class, and seven or more, though often stimulating to teach, need a lot of room and a longer lesson if adequate instruction is to be given.

2. THE LENGTH OF THE LESSON

This is very rarely in the power of the teacher to decide. With a class of four to six I have found forty to forty-five minutes comfortable, but thirty-five minutes a scramble, while thirty minutes is impossible if an adequate amount of ground is to be covered in the course of the lesson. Unpacking and tuning may well take ten minutes, packing up another five, which leaves a fairly small proportion of teaching time. For this reason I feel a class of seven or more should have fifty minutes to an hour.

One other factor should be borne in mind. If the class consists of very young children their concentration is usually fairly short-lived and, therefore, an actual teaching time of twenty minutes is possibly enough. Older children can concentrate for longer periods.

3. CHOOSING THE PUPILS

It is a very lucky instrumental teacher indeed who can choose his pupils, especially in the cello group. Too often he is presented with four or five youngsters who have come along 'because Mr. X says we need cellists in the school orchestra and I've got big hands', 'because Mother (or Father) wants me to' (rare in these days), 'because my best friend learns', or perhaps, by a real stroke of good fortune, 'because I've always wanted to learn the cello'.

Interest and curiosity can be aroused if the music teacher or the head will arrange for the cello teacher to visit several classes, play the instrument to them, and talk quite informally about it, answering any questions and then pointing out that there is a chance for them to learn. If some sort of hand-out is available for interested children to take home to their parents, giving details of cost of lessons (if any), instrument availability (whether or when they will be expected to hire or buy a cello), and any other conditions, such as how long they must learn before they can withdraw from the group, then misconceptions at home due to garbled versions of the day's demonstration can be avoided. A specimen of this type of form and of a parents' agreement form is given at the end of the chapter.

If enough interest is stimulated the teacher may be in the happy position of being able to select pupils. Alternatively he may be asked by the school music teacher what are the desirable qualities in a would-be cellist. Some of my ideas on this may seem surprising, but they are based on long experience.

(i) *A reasonable ear, especially for low notes.* I do not place much emphasis on a child's ability to sing in tune, as quite a few children can hear well, but cannot, for various reasons, pitch well. A would-be cellist should, however, be able to tell whether semitones played slowly on the C string are rising or falling in pitch and should, I think, be able to recognize their own National Anthem, or perhaps the latest hit-tune.

(ii) *Broad, strong hands.* Miss Gertrude Collins advocates shaking hands with all would-be violinists to see how strong their grip is. This is an excellent plan, but with cellists strength is not enough ; hands must be broad, there must be no webbing between the fingers, and it is better that finger-tips should be broad. Children with double-jointed fingers should be discouraged, although I have known one or two who have been so keen and intelligent that they have over-come this particular disability sufficiently to become reasonable amateur cellists and get a great deal of enjoy-ment out of playing.

If the child is still very small it is reasonable to look at his or her feet; if they are large the child (and the hands) will probably grow large enough in due course!

(iii) *Good home background.* While it is usually possible to borrow or hire a cello for a time, sooner or later the pupil should have one of his own. The instrument, even a modern mass-produced one, is not likely to cost less than £60 and will probably be much more. In addition, it will have to be carried around, and parents with cars, especially in rural areas, are useful though not a necessity! As with everything else, though, it is parental encouragement and co-operation with the teacher which is most help of all. It is impossible to rate too highly those parents who realize that learning to play will take a long time; that practice, even if painful to both sides, is essential; and that interest and sympathy work wonders.

(iv) *A sense of humour.* Most children who learn stringed instruments suffer agonies from teasing, not only from other children, but from thoughtless adults. Aunts, uncles, railway ticket collectors, bus conductors (who are often rude as well), indeed anyone who asks whether they 'play it under their chin', or 'use it as a hatstand', seem to regard cellists struggling with their totally unwieldy instruments as fair game. In addition, when it has to be carried on a train or bus, many people take the line that 'it ought not to be allowed', as if anyone—let alone a youngster—enjoyed trying to protect a fragile instrument in the hurly burly of public transport or the school bus. A really sensitive child will often refuse to go on learning for this reason alone, but really sensitive children usually make the best musicians. A sense of humour will help tide over the worst effects of this kind of thoughtlessness from other people.

(v) *The ability to work hard.* This may be very difficult to assess, as there may be nothing in the rest of the child's school work to indicate his ability to work at the cello. Quite often, indeed, a suddenly awakened interest in a musical instrument in a child who seems dull and backward will start a chain reaction which will push his academic work up to, and above, the level of his classmates. I once started a pupil who, academically, was a year behind his age group, and lagging. His progress on the instrument was such that he gained confidence in everything else and had caught up and passed his contemporaries within a year.

(vi) *Intelligence.* Most people would be surprised to see this placed so low in the list and of course there is nothing so enjoyable as teaching a really intelligent pupil—provided he is also musical. But as intelligent children get older the pressures on them become acute. There are examinations, with the possibility of University Entrance or other requirements looming ominously. They are usually good at everything; they may well be good at sport, in the first eleven or the tennis team, or represent the school in athletics. They probably belong to several clubs, possibly including the time-consuming dramatic society. They will probably be picked for positions of responsibility such as prefect, captain of games, house captain. All these things take time, spare time, time when practice could be fitted in, and I have often found that the instrument is crowded out, just when it is most essential for future pleasure that lessons should continue. A good teacher can ease a pupil over this period, but it takes skill and understanding.

(vii) *Keenness.* Again, this may seem an odd factor to put last, but I have found it to be so variable and so dependent on outside stimulation that one cannot rely on it. Every child likes trying something new, but unfortunately the cello, like every other musical instrument, cannot be learnt without hard work, self-discipline, and a great deal of drudgery. The school should know the children who try everything for two weeks and then lose interest and should discourage these from starting. Children and parents should be clearly informed that they must learn for at least a term (it may be possible to insist on a year) and that due notice must be given of withdrawal from a class, in a suitable note from the parents. Parents should sign a form saying that they understand these conditions, and I append a specimen of the kind of thing at the end of the chapter.

With every child the first keenness is bound to wear off, and as new and more difficult techniques are encountered there will be periods of frustration and depression, perhaps despair. I have tried to suggest some ways of countering this in Chapter 10, as I have found it a very real problem, not only as a teacher, but in my own student days.

To end on a lighter note: I have in the course of my teaching life received many excuses from children who wished to stop. The following were not only unforgettable, but also made me think:

'Dear Miss,

Please can Marlene stop the violin today as she is starting music lessons on Saturday.'

'Dear Miss,

I am not doing the cello any more as Mum says cooking will do me more good.'

Possible form to be sent to parents when instrumental classes are to be formed.

Group Tuition is available in school in the following instruments:

. . . .

Lessons will cost . . . . per term.
or Lessons will be free
and an instrument may be borrowed (hired) from the school for an initial period of one year. If your child makes good progress then you might have to purchase an instrument for him/her later on. If you are interested, would you return the form below to us?
It does not commit you to anything.

Name of child . . . .   Age . . . .

Address . . . .

School . . . .

My child is interested in learning an instrument. He/She would prefer *(give name of instrument)*.
May I have further details?

Signed . . . . (Parent or Guardian).

SECOND FORM

This should set out the exact terms on which the lessons are arranged: how many in a term, the exact charge, what happens if the child misses lessons through illness, who is responsible for the instrument, who pays for string replacements, and who pays for damage if this is incurred off the school premises. It should also state quite clearly the requirements about notice.

One we used for many years is reproduced here. Two copies should be sent so that the parent may retain one.

SPECIMEN FORM

GROUP RULES AND FEES
Group Fees

Groups of three pupils (30 minutes)
1st Rate .. BEGINNERS .. £2.00 per term of 10 lessons. (Fees will be increased to 2nd rate in the September following the commencement of lessons.)

2nd Rate .. .. £3.00 per term of 10 lessons. (Where schools have a 40 minute timetable a group should consist of four pupils.)

Shared Lessons
For *two* pupils (30 minutes) .. £4.00 per term of 10 lessons.
Hire of instruments .. .. 50p per term.
Use of music supplied .. .. 10p per term.

Group Rules

(i)   *Fees* are payable for lessons missed, unless the student is away over a period because of illness, or for any other unavoidable reason, in which case half a term's fees will be charged.

(ii)   *Instruments.* When no longer required it is the responsibility of the hirers to see that their instruments are returned to the school (clearly labelled). Until the instrument is received at the office the hire fees will continue to be charged.

(iii)   *Termination of Lessons.* The school term consists of not less than 10 weeks. Any student wishing to discontinue lessons may do so by giving *one month's notice in writing before the end of term*; otherwise a further half term's fee will be charged in lieu of notice.

At the bottom the parent should sign a form of indemnity of this kind:

I have read, understand, and accept the conditions set out above and have kept the duplicate form for reference. I wish my child to learn the instrument mentioned below.

Name of child ....

Address ....

School........................... Age ......

Instrument ....

Signature of Parent or Guardian ....

3 Planning the Work

Too many instrumental lessons begin with the words 'Now, what did we do last week?' Provided the teacher has an overall plan and knows the answer to his question it is a very sensible one to ask. It can be a good way of finding out whether the necessary practice has been done in between lessons. But it usually means that the teacher does not know the answer, has no overall plan, and has done no preparation for the lesson. This way lies frustration, boredom, and frequent chaos.

There should first of all be an overall long-term plan. The teacher should know where he is going and the route he is going to use, even if he cannot time the journey—and this is quite impossible because speeds vary according to age, or aptitude, or even the character of any given group.

The outline scheme suggested later in this chapter is based on the use of certain fingers or finger patterns in a logical sequence, so that the group is presented with each concept in order, and difficulties are introduced one at a time. The order of finger patterns is to some extent based on the personal preference of the teacher, but the one suggested here is advocated for the following reasons:

(i) It brings the left hand round to the correct position quickly and naturally.

(ii) It means that cellists learn notes in the keys of D and A major early in their career, and so can join in with element-ary violinists, who do most of their early work in these keys (see Chapters 9 and 10).

When the pupil has completed Stage III the teacher must decide whether to complete the fingering for first position or teach fourth position and half position. This will depend on many factors—personal preference, the size of the children's hands in relation to their cellos, the music currently needed for the school orchestra, and so on. The problems and advantages of teaching extended positions before fourth position are discussed fully in Chapter 6.

The essential part of planning is to keep a feeling of progression in the lessons. Nothing is more depressing to pupils or teacher than to feel that they are stuck. The solution may lie in introducing new music, perhaps rather easier so that it can be learnt quickly and with a sense of achievement, or pushing on to a new stage in the teaching, or turning to ensemble work for a few weeks to give variety. Long pieces should be avoided in group work whenever possible. They occupy too much of the lesson, making variety within the available time difficult to attain, and children in the early stages find them boring to practise.

It is vitally important that the teacher should make a plan for each lesson, based on the previous week's attainment (or lack of it), and related to the overall syllabus for the term. This weekly lesson plan must be written down so that it can be referred to at any time before, during, or after the lesson. It is best to keep a notebook for this purpose and to make a note also of the work set for practice.

Each lesson should include technical work, aural training, any necessary theory and, if possible, sight reading, as well as the pieces which will be the basis of the teaching. The teacher's notes for the lesson must record in detail each of these aspects, e.g. what type of exercise, which scales, what theory, as well as the pieces.

There should be a provisional timetable in the teacher's

mind. It is too easy to spend twenty-five minutes getting a scale correct and to find that urgent work needed on pieces has to be skimped, while aural training is omitted altogether. It may be necessary to work intensively on one or two bars of a piece before playing it through and a note, kept from the previous lesson, of passages which caused difficulty at that time will often be the key to the planning of the next lesson.

Inevitably the proposed timing for each session must be flexible since it is quite impossible to anticipate exactly how much progress the children will make from week to week, but it is very important indeed that the lesson should have impetus and progression. In this respect the remarks under note (vi) at the end of the chapter are particularly important.

At the end of the lesson each child should leave with written instructions (on the music or in a notebook) about practising. Not only which scales, pieces, and passages, but also how long to practise each day should be indicated, so that parents and, if necessary, other teachers in the school may know exactly what is expected.

Everything in the lesson should be interrelated and the teacher must learn to avoid 'red herrings'. I once heard a teacher asked about the bass clef go on to describe the treble clef and the C clefs. At the end of his dissertation the bell rang and the children (who had obviously done no practice anyway) departed, greatly pleased with their diversionary tactics. Technical work should be related both to the music being studied at the moment (for instance the scales and arpeggios in the keys of the various pieces) and to pieces that will be introduced in a few weeks' time. For instance, a very elementary group might be approaching the 'Russian Dance' from *Twenty Tunes for Beginners* (Palmer

and Best). Before bow and fingers are put together the bowing exercise (Ex. 1) would need to be practised on all strings

Ex.1

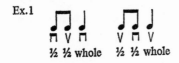

½ ½ whole   ½ ½ whole

and indeed across the strings. Or if slurred bowing is in the
offing this sort of exercise, taught by rote, can be usefully
introduced (cf. also Chap. 4), Ex. 2a first, followed a week
or two later by Ex. 2b.

Ex.2a)   Ex.2b)

Similar principles apply in aural training. The recognition of the interval of a 5th, and of which string is which, is
essential at the very first stage, followed by interval training
and rhythm training. Half-a-term before introducing
minor scales, aural work on major and minor intervals and
the recognition of the difference is essential.

Attention to key signatures is crucial well before any
new finger pattern is introduced. Children must know that
third finger on A string plays C *sharp*, that third on D
plays F *sharp* and that these notes are required because of the
sharps at the beginning of the piece. At the same time it is
best to avoid teaching concepts that they will not need for
another year or so. This becomes purely theoretical and can
be a complete waste of lesson time.

Liaison with the school music teacher can help in all these
things. It is important to know how theory of music is taught
(if at all) in each school. One teacher may use tonic solfa,
another straight notation. One may use French time-names,

another words for rhythm-patterns, another a mainly mathematical approach. In any case, children will often not associate the music taught in the classroom with the cello lesson. (I once spent fifteen valuable minutes trying to teach a cello class the meaning of $\frac{6}{8}$. They were quite adamant that they had never heard of it; when their music mistress arrived and suggested to them that their previous lesson with her had been almost entirely concerned with the same thing they said, 'Oh, but that was *music*: this is *cello*!')

The outline lesson plan given below is based on the rule that each lesson should end with a feeling of achievement. There are occasional lessons when the rule can be broken, but these should be rare. One occasion may be when the teacher wishes to anticipate something totally new which will be introduced in the next lesson, either by playing himself or introducing it in some pleasurable way. Another, when the group has been slack and no one has practised, is to give a bread-and-butter lesson on basics, incorporating in it a session on how to practise. Too few pupils know how to practise and far too few teachers teach the techniques of practising—an art which is rarely acquired instinctively. This kind of lesson should be really hard grinding work and the purpose should be made quite clear: 'You haven't practised properly, if at all, so we must do it now, and this is how you must do it in future.' If, when the group gets outside the door, the teacher hears an exhausted groan, he may take it that the lesson has been a success. But it should only happen very occasionally.

The notes attached to the outline scheme of the lesson given below are very important, particularly the first and last. Nothing can be hard and fast—except the school bell if there is one.

SPECIMEN OUTLINE PLAN OF LESSON

1. Technical work: bowing, scales, arpeggios, etc., relating to work in the lesson or future work.
2. Half-learned piece.
3. Sight-reading (very short).
4. New piece—introduction, reading through part, dealing with difficulties.
5. Aural training.
6. Polishing a better-known piece.
7. Quick summary of practising expected in the following week.

Notes on this plan

(i)   Timing is essential: deduct at least ten minutes from the overall lesson time if cellos have to be taken out of cases, tuned, and then put away at the end of the lesson. Have a clear idea of how much time you will spend on each section of the lesson. *Never teach without a watch or clock.*

(ii)   Always aim at ending at least three minutes before the bell is due. This will give a little extra time for discussion or clearing up. Clearing up in a hurry always leads to disaster.

(iii)   Give the pupils, especially the young ones, some rest from the physically exhausting playing by using aural training, etc., as a game.

(iv)   A new piece will not be desirable at every lesson, especially as work gets more difficult. It is best to deal with any major problems early in the lesson while the children are fresh.

(v)   Keep a notebook handy, and note in it what you achieved and what went wrong (a simple code of $\sqrt{}$ and $\times$ will deal with this, plus the odd note of particular difficulties encountered by any one of the group).

(vi)   Be prepared to vary a lesson. It is fatal to start every lesson in the same way. If everyone is becoming stale, start occasionally with sight-reading, or give an ensemble lesson, or play to the class yourself. Sooner or later every teacher will be confronted with a totally unforeseen situation—a different room, a bulldozer outside the window, a broken string or bow, a damaged instrument or one left behind on the school bus, lost music, visitors . . . the list is endless. In this sort of situation improvisation and quick thinking are essential and carefully thought-out plans must be abandoned for that week. But it is still essential to make a note of what has been done.

4 The Stages in Detail—Stage I

Basic Principles. In all that follows two basic principles are implied if not always expressed:

(i) Never ask the class to tackle more than one difficulty at a time.

(ii) Teach each new point by rote and example first.

The first playing lesson

N.B. The teacher should have met the children once to sort out names and faces, allocate or measure them for the right size cellos as far as possible, and tell them what they must expect and what will be expected of them. It may be possible to incorporate a little of what I have included in the following suggested lesson into that meeting, but circumstances will dictate how far things can go. In effect, the first playing lesson may very well be the second lesson of term. If storage space is available in school it is much better not to allow pupils to take the instruments home until they can handle them with some certainty. No great harm will come if no practice is done for the first few lessons. After that practice must be arranged either at school or at home.

1. *Room arrangement.* The matter of space was dealt with at some length in Chapter 1. If possible the teacher should arrange the room for the first lesson before the class arrives, seat them as he wants them, and restrain them from moving the chairs, which will be placed far apart. The instinct of every class is to huddle together for safety (or reassurance)

and it will be a constant battle to keep chairs well separated. Possible arrangements are shown as follows:

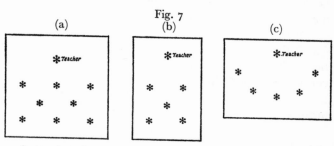

Fig. 7

(a)   (b)   (c)

Suggestions for seating of group in rooms of various shapes

No stands are allowed for at this stage. I prefer to use charts for the first two terms (less clutter in the classroom and easier to keep the class together), and so every child must be able to see the teacher and the charts.

2. Give out the cellos in canvas cases if possible. The teacher also has one in a canvas case. By example he shows the class how to 'undress' the cello, *being careful to make everyone remove the bows and put them in a safe place first.*

3. Canvas cases are put by the chairs; the pupils sit down with their cellos across their knees (or held diagonally upwards if there is very little space), pull out the spike to about a hand-and-a-half's-span, and tighten the screw.

4. The teacher shows all the children how to sit and then goes to each child individually to adjust the length of the spike. It is important to try to make comments to everyone while doing this; it may take time, it is *very* important that everyone should understand what is being done, and the class can get out of hand at this point if great care is not exercised.

Points to watch in adjusting spikes:

(i)   Is the chair the right height (see Chapter 1)? Much can be done where chairs are too low, less when chairs are too high.

(ii) Is the pupil on the front of the chair?

(iii) Is the scroll over the left shoulder?

(iv) Is the cello at a reasonable angle?

(v)   Is the left lower back bout sticking into the pupil's left knee-cap (or thereabouts) and is the front table of the instrument about 5 cm. higher than the right knee-cap?

5.   The children are encouraged to pluck the strings with right hand three-quarters of the way down the fingerboard and thumb against the side of the fingerboard (see Plate 3). I ask them to start from their left (usually I say 'window' side, 'door' side, etc. as they never know left from right) and play each string twice. Establish first which is highest and which lowest in pitch and then teach the names.

6.   Play each string four times, perhaps with an accompaniment, saying the letter names.

7.   Suggest they make up words on the letter names for next time (this can be their practice). There are not many words, but ADD, CAD, GAG, DAD, can be used.

8.   Put down the cellos, pick up the bows, and show the group how to screw and unscrew. Then hold the middle of the stick with the left hand, point pointing left, hair towards floor, bow level with tummy and encourage them to drop the right hand on to the stick 'like a bunch of bananas', with the thumb bent in. (See Plates 4a, 4b, and 4c.)

9.   Put down the bows, pick up the cellos to check the playing position, and perhaps pluck again.

10.   Get them to guess with their eyes shut which string the teacher is playing (if their cellos are still in tune they can try to echo after the teacher).

11. Again watching the teacher, pack the cellos and bows in the canvas cases and practise carrying them round the room. (This will take eight to ten minutes if done properly.)

This is enough material for a very long lesson. I frequently omit all bow handling from the first lesson except for a warning on fragility. Do not leave out all the playing—this is too frustrating for the children.

Following on the first lesson the teacher must complete Stage IA of the outline plan. I prefer to show the written symbols for the notes (in crotchets) as early as possible. Again, this is debatable, but with very young children the use of charts and a different colour for each string helps very considerably if the teacher wishes to introduce notation at an early stage.

The second and subsequent lessons must contain work on the bow. Once the bow is correctly held then manipulative exercises can follow.

1. Holding the bow in the right hand *but still at stomach level* swing the point of the stick in and out, making the first and little fingers exert pressure on the bow alternately. This is *not* an up and down swing—the bow must move parallel with the floor.

2. With the cello in playing position, put the bow on the D string half-way between fingerboard and bridge, with the stick masking the hair from the player (i.e., tilted towards the fingerboard). Move the bow until the point is resting on the string and then steady it there, at right angles to the string, with the left hand. Now move the right hand along the stick keeping the thumb bent. This can be repeated on all strings and gives the pupil a feeling of the planes along which the right hand will have to travel on each string. It may also help to relax the hand on the bow.

3. Ask the pupil, holding the bow in the normal correct way, to place the middle of the hair on G string half-way between bridge and fingerboard. Now, without moving the bow laterally, swing it back (*not* down) until it rests on the C string and then forward (*not* up) until it rests on the A string. This whole process should be soundless as the bow rests and pivots on the strings and is not drawn along them.

The reason for the emphasis on swinging back and forward lies in the angle of the bow in relation to the cello strings. The bow must always cross the strings at right angles and to the player this looks as if he bows behind him on the C string and right out in front on the A string (often a long stretch which beginners find impossible). I often draw pencil lines on the upper side of the cello bridge to help the players thus:

Fig. 8

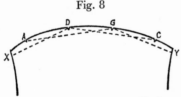

Diagram to show lines which can be pencilled on cello bridge to help a pupil obtain correct bow angles

(We are looking down on the bridge from above towards the floor).

The bow on the A string will follow the line X–D, on the D string the line A–G, on the G string the line D–C, and on the C string the line G–Y.

If players are still in difficulty over this I use a landmark: 'Bow towards the door, or the cupboard, or Billy's chair', etc. Pupils should be encouraged to swing the trunk of the body while bowing, particularly on the A string, without altering the basic seating position.

4. This bowing angle is very difficult to impress upon the pupil and constant care must be exercised to get it right. A further exercise (still soundless) is to make the pupil lift the bow and place the point and the heel alternately in the same spot on each string, gradually increasing the speed.

5. When the exercises are established long straight bows may be tried on each string in turn, emphasizing the need for the correct angle and for sounding only one string at once. If a pupil has a short arm and cannot reach the point and keep the bow straight, a white tape mark can be placed on the stick at an appropiate place to act as a substitute 'point'. The child will then be told to bow only as far as the tape.

STAGE IB

This stage can be entered on fairly quickly. It may be that left hands are very weak, and if this is so exercises to strengthen them can be used to rest the pupils and bring an element of fun into the lesson. Most teachers will have their own favourites, but I have found these useful:

(i) Holding hands up, palms towards face, bend each finger in turn without moving the others, and then two at a time.

(ii) With hands in the same position and fingers a little apart, move each finger in turn sideways so that it touches its neighbours on either side.

(iii) Rest the finger-tips of the left hand lightly on desk or table top (or cello ribs) and bend the joint nearest the nail of each finger in and out, each by itself and quite independently. (This is a marvellous exercise.)

(iv) With the cello in playing position, and the ball of the

left thumb slightly to the left side of the neck, anywhere
between scroll and body, pluck the A or D string with the
left-hand first finger and then bang it down on the same
string immediately. This should be a reflex action and if
the finger has fallen freely and on its tip a satisfying 'ping' of
recognizable pitch should result. Most children cannot
make a sound at first! When the first finger scores a success
the pupil plucks with No. 2 and bangs down in quick
succession one and two on the same string. When the third
finger plucks, one, two, and three are banged down in turn
(weight being transferred to each finger), and by the time
the fourth finger plucks the player should have a definite
sensation of rolling weight from first to little finger as each
bangs down after the other.

The correct position for the first finger of the left hand
can now be taught. I find it helpful to put a wad of sellotape
on the neck of the cello, slightly to the outside, to mark
where the ball of the left thumb should lie. To do this the
teacher must hold each cello properly, note where his thumb
comes (slightly nearer the floor of course than the first
finger), mark the spot with a pencil, and then stick the wad
on. It does not harm the cello and is most useful for children
who find it difficult to hear the correct pitch to begin with
—or who forget about that aspect of playing in the morass
of other difficulties.

With or without the wad the group should be told to sit
up straight behind their cellos, swing their left arms straight
out to shoulder level, and then bend them at the elbow so
that the thumbs fall on the neck of the cello and the fingers
fall loosely on the D string. This is where the sellotape
wad is so useful: if the thumb is on it there is a reasonable
chance that the first finger will be fairly well in tune and the
note can be played by each child in turn and corrected.

It is *essential* that the children should not look at their left hands. If they do, the neck of the cello will be pushed away from their own necks and a bad playing position will result. They can check each other (in pairs), and a mirror is useful, but otherwise the position must be found by feeling and listening. I suggest the D string to begin with because it is still easy to hear and the correct left elbow position is more easily attained than on the A. (See Plates 5a, 5b, and 5c.)

Once the first finger position is established then simple exercises can be taught by rote, such as Ex. 2, and finally the names of the notes can be shown and notation taught.

Simple aural games can be played ('eyes shut—which notes are these?' 'now imitate it', 'is that in tune?') to encourage the listening aspect, but at all times the whole group must be involved. Simple pieces, using open strings and first finger, can now be learnt, and it is important to include some for C string although these notes are much more difficult to hear. They are also much more difficult to read and children get lazy about them.

Meanwhile, bowing continues. Simple rhythms on open strings are essential, and if these can be fitted to words so much the better. 'Hot Cross Buns' is most useful, and I teach it in two stages: the first

Ex.3a)

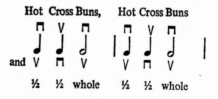

then, considerably later,

Ex. 3b)

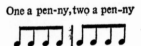

($\frac{1}{4}$ bow at the nut or point according to the start of the whole exercise).

Another is

Ex.3c)

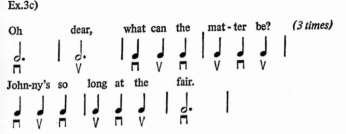

Yet another rhythm (make your own words),

Ex.3d)

and more will be found in most cello tutors. But I do find that children get bored to tears with lines of dull-looking exercises and will not practise them. So the teacher must constantly be thinking of new ideas. One game I play with all my groups is a variation of the slow bicycle race. The children are asked to keep their bows going in one direction on a given string for as long as possible. If the bow stops at all, that is cheating, and they are 'out'. The teacher starts them and then counts steadily. Some children can keep a down bow or up bow going for twenty-five or thirty seconds, and I always find that this piece of technique is practised even by the child who is otherwise making no headway at all! This slow bowing will often counteract a tendency to raise the right elbow too high and to tighten muscles in the upper arm which must be relaxed. I often suggest that they must feel as if they had a heavy shopping bag hanging from their right elbow weighing it down; an imaginative suggestion like this will often help, especially with young children.

As soon as some measure of bow control is achieved they should begin bowing the simple open-string pieces they plucked in the earlier lessons.

STAGE IC

It is important to get a good left-hand position established as soon as possible. From now on the group will need constant reminders about keeping their left elbow out, keeping their fingers round, and keeping the fingers on their tips. For children with rather thin finger-tips this is difficult, but they can be reassured that tips will broaden in time.

It is at this moment too that the fight over long finger-nails tends to begin, especially with girls. Ultimately a decision has to be taken between playing the cello and having long nails (all too often the nails win), but at this stage gentle persuasion and constant reminder may well do the trick. It is a good idea for a teacher to carry a pair of sharp nail scissors, but only to lend to a pupil, *never* to operate himself. Charges of assault have been brought by infuriated parents on such grounds.

Good and bad elbow and hand positions are illustrated
in Plates 5a, 5b, and 5c.

In a good position the elbow should be out, with the thumb
on the outer side of the neck between the first and second
fingers, and the fingers rounded and on their tips.

To get this it is important to teach a scale, plucked and
by rote, as soon as possible. Too much time spent on open
string and first finger means that the other fingers get lazy
and fall away under the fingerboard and this quickly
becomes a habit very difficult to cure; so it is better to
prevent it.

I teach first the scale of G major—one octave plucked,
each note twice ascending. Not until they can imitate me
with a fair degree of accuracy do I teach the descending
scale and then I encourage a pause to think before putting
down all four fingers on the lower string. It may well be
that the ascending scale is taught one week, the descending
a week or more later and the pause to think not eliminated
for three or four weeks. If some of the class find the scale
comparatively easy and others are still struggling, I make
the ascending scale more difficult for them by telling them
to anchor the fingers on the lower string until they need
them on the upper string. This is excellent for a good hand
position, difficult but not impossible to do, and will keep
them fully occupied while the less competent pupils struggle.
In the same way children can be encouraged in the descending scale to lift fingers across towards the lower string.

Once the scale has been taught the notation may be
shown and simple pieces using 1–3 and 1–3.4 fingers
introduced. I use very few 1–3 pieces as I find that the
excitement of playing a tune they know will more than offset
any extra notational difficulty. (Some children will play by
ear anyway and this is good provided they can be made to

read notation as well at some stage.) Any tune that lies within the octave scale will do, provided it is rhythmically simple: 'Twinkle, twinkle, little star', 'Now the day is over', and 'Cock-a-doodle doo' are tunes that I have found endlessly useful, and there are many more. A major advantage is that both the child and his parents (if practice is done at home) know what the 'end product' should sound like! For a pupil with no musical background at all this is very important in the early stages.

In bowing at this stage I concentrate on trying to obtain some flexibility. Very often the pupil is clutching the bow as if it was made of gold and might be snatched at any moment. Two exercises can help here. Children can be told to rest the right arm against the cello, rest the bow on the string, and, without moving the arm, move the bow an inch or two using wrist and fingers only. This is a very tiring exercise and must be only used for a very short time. The second is another bowing exercise, to the rhythm of 'Jack and Jill':

Ex.4

The class is told to flick the up bow, and so to time the bowing that 'water' comes in the last four inches of the bow. I sometimes say 'down, flick, down, flick, down, flick, down, flick', etc., and make it quite clear that the flick only recovers a small distance of the down bow stroke which in itself was probably about four inches. The idea of different bow speeds can also be introduced at this stage in an elementary way, still using open strings: rhythms such as

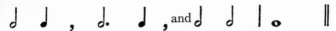

all using whole bows, should be encouraged, with the children eventually counting as they play.

More complicated open string pieces will be followed by the great moment when left hand and right hand are joined. It is advisable to give the simplest possible exercise by rote first: the following is an example:

Ex.5

Each note is played twice so that the change of finger comes on a down bow, which is rhythmically more natural. This can be followed (if all goes well) by the notes played once each. Usually open string and first finger pieces are so well written that no more preliminaries are needed. The class will have learnt the piece pizzicato in an earlier lesson and can proceed to the right bowing.

Aural work at this time can be based on the scales. The tests used in early Associated Board examinations are good—recognition of the degree of the scale played by the teacher and singing the degree of the scale after being given the key-note. These can be used as games in class and will very often serve as a useful rest for class and teacher alike. Clapping of simple rhythms in a 'follow-my-leader' way is also good fun and a most useful exercise.

4

Now comes a period of consolidation which may well last a
term or two. If things are rushed now there may well be an
insecure base and trouble later: on the other hand it may
well be counter-productive to wait until the slowest member
of the class is really good at the work. The teacher may, in
the interest of the majority, have to grit his teeth and go on,
giving a little extra time to the child who is behind, or
transferring him back to a lower class if one is available.
On the other hand, one bright child in a slow class may also
need special attention, or transfer to a more advanced
group.

Once the pizzicato scale is established bowing should
follow as soon as possible. Again, two bows to a note are
advisable to begin with (cf. Ex. 6a), followed by one to a
note with the key-note repeated at the top, and all even
notes—cf. Ex. 6b:

Ex.6a)

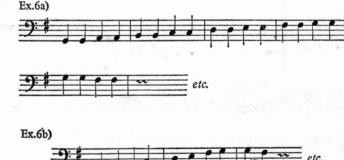

etc.

Ex.6b)

etc.

The one-octave scales C, G, and D (all starting on the open
string), should be covered, especially C major. The notation
of this needs special emphasis as there is a shortage of pieces

involving C string notes and much practice is needed on them.

One-octave arpeggios can also be taught at this stage, plucked first and then bowed, and again it is useful to make as many pupils as possible keep third fingers down as long as they can.

Ex.7

Hold 3rd. finger down

All pieces learnt should still be in the same finger pattern, but can become increasingly complicated rhythmically and technically. They should still be taught pizzicato first and any technical difficulties anticipated in advance by simple exercises. For instance, supposing one was going to teach 'Cock a doodle-doo' in C major:

Ex.8a)

suitable exercises in previous weeks could be:

(1) Arpeggio of C major.

(2) **Ex.8b)**

to anticipate the bowing need in bars four and seven.

At the same time musical playing should be emphasized. Bowing exercises for *p* and *f* should be given, and I find a particularly popular one (on open strings at this stage) is the following:

Ex.9

This can later be transferred to the scales.

STAGE IE

By this time children should be familiar with the sounds and fingerings of the first finger-pattern and the teacher will begin to move towards the second finger-pattern in aural and theory work. This must be done very subtly by reference to what is being done rather than what is to come, and meanwhile certain other technical points should be covered.

Scales and arpeggios should by now be familiar, so I encourage the class to play in canon. The result at first is usually appalling, but it is amazing how quickly the children get the idea and improve and check their intonation.

Scale (top key-note played *once* only)

Ex.10

The moment of truth is at X which should be in unison. Once this is pointed out the children will quickly realize what to look for and get it right. Furthermore, they will practise in order to be able to do this as a duet.

Arpeggios, which can of course be played in three or four parts if necessary, can be similarly treated.

Ex.11

Slurred bowing must also be tackled at this time. I prefer to leave it until now and apply it to the scale; some people like to apply it to open strings very much earlier. This is a matter of opinion. I tackle it in this way:

Ex.12

The children are told to play half a down bow and then stop, put down the first finger and continue in the same direction. The teacher demonstrates the appropriate moves on his instrument first, and then with the children. When this is sorted out (and some children find it *very* difficult) they are told to cut out the stop:

Ex.13a)

When this is conquered they proceed to

Ex.13b)

(no string crossing involved).

Then they are ready for the whole scale:

Ex.13c)

I prefer to teach this form to start with as it cuts out the very nasty string cross involved in the slurred scales asked for by the Associated Board, *viz*:

Ex.13d)

Once the principle is learnt on the easier scale form there is little difficulty in changing over. Slurring three and four to a bow can be taught initially by short exercises similar to Example 13a above.

Finally, at this stage it is important to teach the change of bow hold involved in plucking and bowing. This can be taught earlier if necessary, but it *must be taught*.

The following method works well.

(i) Demonstrate how to change the hold:

    (a) hold bow normally,

    (b) slide fingers under frog and bring thumb out, turning the stick so that the base of the frog is towards palm of hand,

    (c) put thumb against the fingerboard and pluck with first finger.

(ii) Drill this way several times.

(iii) Now ask them to play a scale very slowly bowing and plucking each note in turn.

Ex. 14

Make sure that they do the change properly each time.

(iv) Send them away to practise and see who can do it fastest —only proper changes accepted!

The result next lesson is usually 100% correct at an astonishing speed.

All these techniques should be applied to pieces as soon as possible and should be taught with specific pieces in view.

By this time the difference in speed of progress between pupils in the group will be fairly obvious (unless the teacher has been exceptionally lucky), and there will also be times when a child must be heard on his own. The thing to avoid *at all costs* is to have five children sitting idle while the teacher attends to the sixth. The five will not be idle for long and, what is worse, may become bored and frustrated as well.

I therefore list some dodges which I have found useful:

(i) The child doing best (or worst) points to the chart while the others play. If time permits they can all have a go. (This often reveals difficulties in note reading which are illuminating to the teacher; for instance, rests may be ignored altogether.)

(ii) Each child is allocated one or two bars and the piece is then played through and must sound as if one person is playing it: 'keep the pot boiling'. In this case all the class must be encouraged to 'ghost'-play the bars they are not actually playing properly and it is often a good idea, if one or more bars are left over (in an eight bar tune and a group of six playing one bar each two bars will be 'spare'), to say 'Everyone joins in the last two bars'. This is often difficult to work at first and it is well worth the extra effort required to insist that everybody 'ghosts' all the time. Furthermore, one can always see that a child having difficulty with one bar has to play that bar, or alternatively that a very backward pupil has the simplest bar of the piece.

(iii)   One class member bows, the others pluck.

(iv)   One plays, the others criticize. Beware, here, of the child who is over-sensitive; he can be permanently upset if asked to play something at the wrong moment.

At this stage the aural and theory side are very important. Knowing that new keys and fingerings are in the offing I explain tones and semitones. The order of tones and semitones in a major scale must be learnt and heard. The children must recognize the key-signatures they meet, know to which scale they relate, and which notes are affected by them. More aural work on recognition of intervals, particularly semitones and degrees of the scale is essential. If this is done in very short bursts week after week the ground should be well prepared for the transition to Stage II.

1 *Correct playing position, well forward on chair, feet flat on floor, left elbow well out*

2 *Incorrect playing position, too far back on chair, left foot resting on toe only, left elbow slightly dropped*

3 *Correct position for right hand pizzicato without bow*

4 a *Hand held loosely preparatory to bow-hold*
  b *Hand held loosely for bow-hold and turned towards
    camera to show thumb bent towards second finger*
  c *Position of thumb on bow*
  d *Bow-hold: bow on G string*

a

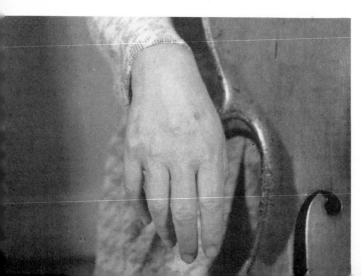

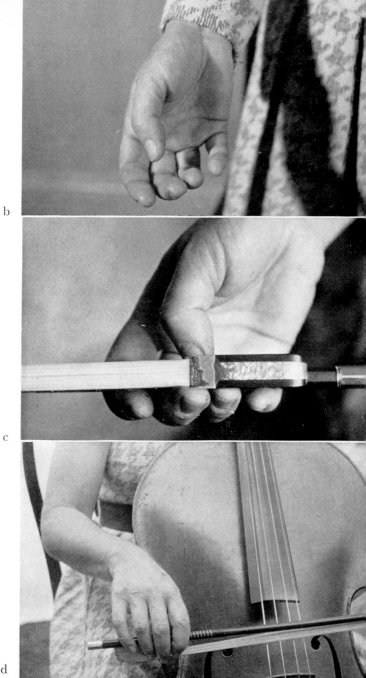

b

c

d

5a *Cello too far
away from
player's neck*

b *Elbow too low
and near centre*

c *Elbow too high,
close to side*

d *Good playing position of left elbow and hand*

e *Badly twisted left hand position, sometimes called 'violinist's twist' : the strained position of the hand is obvious*

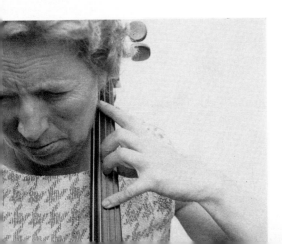

6 *Hand position for extension*

7 *Elbow moved forward and down to facilitate forward extension*

8 *Gap necessary between hand and cello in fourth position*

9a *Practising vibrato on the right arm: view from the front*

b *Practising vibrato on the right arm: position of thumb seen from pupil's right-hand side*

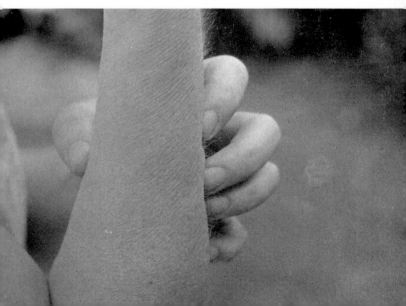

10 *Position of hand in thumb position*

5 The Stages in Detail—Stages II and III

The time spent on this stage should be comparatively short, but it is important to separate it from Stage III in order to confuse the children as little as possible.

The basic technique in this stage is the introduction of a new fingering 0–1. 2–4. To do this I run it alongside finger-pattern one, but keep the lesson carefully divided between the two, usually taking the new finger-pattern first and going back to the old one at the end. To jump to and fro from one to the other will only confuse further what is already complicated from the child's point of view.

To introduce it I usually play a one-octave scale starting on the fourth finger, but using third fingers where second fingers ought to be used, as in Ex. 15.

The resultant peculiar sound should bring a reaction from the children. Some sort of dialogue as this can then take place:

'Is it an ordinary scale?'

'No.'

'Why not?'

(Usual answer) 'You didn't start on an open string.'

'But I meant to start on a fourth finger.' etc., etc., until it is established that the tones and semitones were not in the correct places for a major scale.

I then show them how to make it sound 'right' by using the second finger instead of the third, and they pluck it.

I tend to use F major to begin with because the upper octave of C major can be very confusing in this context.

When the scale is learnt thus we discuss the names of the notes (especially the new notes B♭ and F♮) and look at them. Later top C♮ and low E♭ are introduced. Pieces in this fingering are hard to find but again any tune which lies within the octave scale can be used and it is worth writing out a few hymn tunes, carols, or folk-songs in the appropriate keys (a list is given in the appendix) for use in this way. There is one section in Widdicombe's *40 Folk Tunes for the Cello* (Curwen) which will help here too.

The scales and arpeggios in this finger-pattern can be bowed very quickly and in the second half of the lesson work on scales, arpeggios, and tunes in the first finger-pattern can continue in the normal way. Stress must now be laid at all times on the theoretical and aural side so that the children understand when to use third and when to use second finger.

When the teacher is satisfied that the new principles are understood he can proceed to

STAGE III

This involves the mixing of finger-patterns one and two and the consolidation of all techniques learned so far. The basic scales and arpeggios for this are C major, two octaves, and G major, one octave and a half.

C major, two octaves, can be taught, again by rote, as a combination of finger-patterns one (bottom octave) and two (top octave). It is a good idea to play the two octaves as separate scales repeating the middle key-note thus:

Ex.16

and similarly descending.

The repertoire available in these two finger-patterns is large, since it used to be standard practice to start all pupils on C major, two octaves, and as much practice as possible should be given by using different types of piece, developing not only sense of key but also sense of musicianship.

For the right arm and hand emphasis should be placed on the development of good tone, use of all parts of the bow, and bowings such as stopped short staccato bows, stopped slurred bows, and smooth legato crossing of strings with slurred and separate bows. The type of exercise can be related to scales, arpeggios, or pieces, but should always be related to something. The teacher will probably make his own or use one of the many to be found in the various tutors on the market, but they should be short and should not necessarily need music.

Some examples are:

(1)   **Ex.17**

etc.

Stopped separate bows (a) in middle
                      (b) middle to point
                      (c) nut to middle
                      (d) whole bows

(2)

Ex.18

etc.

Rapid repeated bows (a) at nut
                                   (b) in middle
                                   (c) at point
                                   (d) bounced

All these, of course, can be applied to other strings.

(3)

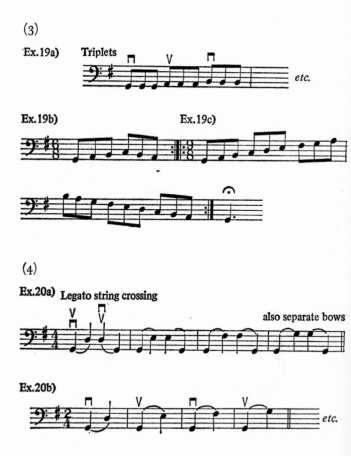

(4)

Ex.20c)

In addition it is important that pupils should know how to play pizzicato chords. There are two ways:

(1) Spread chord   **Ex.21**

Fig. 9a

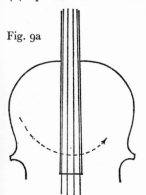

played with right thumb moving in a curve downwards from C string and up again towards A.

(2) Quick chord   **Ex.22**

Fig. 9b

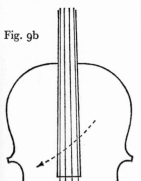

played by first finger (or second) striking diagonally downwards from A string side.

All these should be taught and applied to pieces immediately.

It may well be that pupils at this stage are co-opted into the school orchestra and these points may well be encountered in orchestral parts. Very useful lessons can be given on these parts and the pupils should always be encouraged to bring them to class. In addition liaison with the conductor of the orchestra can often avoid major misunderstandings (see Chapter 9).

The whole of this stage is most important. If the ground has been well covered then the basis for all future development is sound. It is therefore wise to revise with plenty of material, to spend time on sight-reading, ensemble work, and general musicianship, so that the children can play with some confidence.

They should no longer be dependent on charts, but able to follow their own copies, picking up again if they make a mistake.

A good way to check this is for the teacher to play a piece, stop in the middle, and ask whereabouts in the copy he is. Alternatively, he can play a short piece or a couple of lines, make one or two deliberate mistakes and see if they are spotted. (This is a game everyone enjoys.) With a little ingenuity a good deal of rather prosaic work can be made most enjoyable in this way.

To judge when the class should continue to the next stage is a matter of experience and only the teacher can decide. Every class will be different and, whereas with some it may be desirable to go straight on to extensions in the first position (which I myself always prefer), with others it may be much better to continue to fourth position and leave extensions until later. The reasons for this will be discussed in the next chapter. Whatever happens, much emphasis must again be laid on tones and semitones and the structure of the major scale, together with key signatures and their relationship to all the notes and scales learned so far.

6 Backward and Forward Extensions

There are two difficulties, one physical and one mental, involved in teaching extensions. The physical one is fairly obvious—the sheer distance that has to be stretched between first and fourth fingers may seem impossible at first to pupils who have small hands or small, short fingers. A child who is unlucky enough to have webbed fingers may never be able to extend in the orthodox way. The mental difficulty is that all cellists must understand the principle of extensions, why and when they are used, and this implies a knowledge of the theory of music which is, all too often, lacking among the average group member.

The physical difficulty is, in fact, not as great as the non-cellist would think, provided that a correct hand position is secured from the beginning. The hand must be as square to the fingerboard as possible in spite of the stretch, with the first finger pointing straight back towards the shoulder.

If, however, the teacher has doubts about the ability of any member of the group to stretch without straining the hand, then it is wise to leave the teaching of extended positions until after fourth position. Half position can be taught immediately to cover the notes a semitone above each open string. If this order of teaching is adopted then it would be wise to make a special point of getting pupils to bring their orchestral parts to lessons, as judicious editing may well be needed (see Chapter 9).

Up to this stage the class has been taught that each finger of the left hand is placed a semitone apart on the string, the first finger being a tone away from the open string. This means there is an interval of three semitones between first and fourth fingers (i.e. B–D, E–G, A–C, D–F). Pupils are now taught that to get notes which they have not previously played in the first position, they will have to stretch the fingers so that there is an interval of four semitones (two whole tones; i.e., a major third) between first and fourth fingers. As this fingering applies to the first four positions, it is wise to give the group a rule to remember. I usually say, 'Whenever there is a major third between first and fourth fingers (i.e., two whole tones) use an extended position', and I sing the intervals and so do they.

The teacher must check and re-check that the pupils know (a) the sound and (b) the look of a major third and can recognize it on the printed page whenever they see it.

As usual I try to teach the movement, 'feel', and sound of the extension first. A good preliminary exercise (soundless) is to ask the children to find C on the G string with their fourth fingers and then point their first fingers back as far as possible. Any sign of a twisted hand must be corrected immediately.

Very often a child gets into difficulties because he has been gripping the neck of the cello with his left thumb and his hand has become taut. I encourage some movement of the left elbow forward and down and this often helps to release tension. Another relaxing exercise with the hand and elbow in the normal playing position consists of putting all fingers down on one of the strings and stroking the back of the cello neck lightly with the thumb. (The sellotape wad should have been removed by now, but if the instrument is being shared by a more elementary pupil and the wad is still in position it will not interfere with this movement.)

A correct hand position is shown in Plate 6. It will

probably be necessary to drop the elbow forward and down a little as shown in Plate 7.

A kind of scissors movement of the first finger may now be taught. Fingers two, three, and four touch the string lightly (D string for preference), and the pupils are asked to point the first finger back towards the ear and then bring it back to normal playing position, letting it move quite freely. When a free movement is established the fourth finger can be placed firmly on the D string in first position and the first finger moved back on G string until it can play A♭. The D and G strings are easiest to play on in the initial stages since less movement and distortion of the elbow position seem to be necessary.

It is vital to insist on relaxation of the hand in between all these movements. Keen pupils try very hard and get very tense, and it is easy to strain a hand badly while trying to stretch at first.

Once the principle has been grasped the group is introduced to B major scale, one octave, by rote as usual. The fingering is stressed.

Ex.23

(one whole tone between first and second fingers, one whole tone between second and fourth), and the teacher must make it quite clear that the whole hand should not move. He should demonstrate that to reach the E♭ and top B♭ the first finger only should move and should point back as in the exercises, and I have found that it pays to show the children that if the whole hand moves back the G and C are likely to be flat, particularly in the descending scale. It may be possible, after a week or two, to encourage the members of the group who have larger hand spans to hold the C and G down on the ascending scale while the E♭ and top B♭ are played, but this idea must be used sparingly in case over-enthusiastic pupils strain too much. The bottom octave of E♭ major should be taught at this time and it is also useful to point out the alternative notation for the first finger when extended back, i.e.,

Ex.24

The principle of extension fingering—that it is used for successive intervals of two whole tones—must be reiterated over and over again, and applied to the pieces in these keys so that children begin to recognize when to use the fingering.

Again it is wise to begin with a few tunes within the octave which use only extension fingering, proceeding to pieces in F major and B♭ major. Anything in E♭ major tends to incorporate a top A♭, and as this note will only confuse the issue at this stage I prefer to avoid it. At the same time, pieces using normal fingering must also be given (hands can get very tired when extensions are being learnt), and no opportunity missed in pointing out the differences in fingering and the reasons why.

It is at this stage that D minor, G minor, and C minor scales, one octave, may be introduced. Opinions vary as to whether the harmonic or melodic form of minor should be taught first; both have to be taught at some time and there is much to be said for starting with either. Before embarking on minor scales I carry out intensive aural preparation for four or five weeks beforehand, introducing the group to major and minor thirds and trying to ensure that all pupils know and can recognize the difference.

When teaching back extensions, melodic minor scales can be particularly useful, as the emphasis can be placed on the first finger pointing back in the descending scale (see below); but pupils must be watched, in case a twisted hand develops.

Ex.25

If the harmonic form of the minor is taught, emphasis must be placed on the very big stretch of the augmented second, and it may be useful to teach it descending first to avoid the twist developing.

Ex.26

When the movement for backward extension and the principle of the fingering is understood and a reasonable facility has been gained (and this may take some time) the group may be introduced to forward extension. The fingering for this is exactly the same, but all the fingers are one semitone higher. The result is that, unless the teacher takes the greatest care, the children will begin to stretch forward and their hands will again get twisted. The method of counteracting this which is suggested below is controversial but effective in preventing the twist.

The children are told to play G on the D string with the fourth finger, extend the first finger back, so that the hand is in full extended position, and then move the entire hand (thumb included) forward one semitone. The fourth finger should now be playing G♯ and the other fingers F♯ and E. This can be repeated on the G string.

The idea is usually grasped very quickly and I then teach A major and D major scales *descending* from the open string (e.g. Ex. 27A).

Ex.27

A _ _ _ _ _ _ _ _ _ _ _ _ _ _ _ _   B _ _ _ _ _ _ _ _ _ _ _ _ _ _ _ _ _ _

This also comes very easily as the first finger will point back naturally, and the group adds on the ascending half of the scale (B). They must then check on each other's hand positions to see that a twist has not developed. A great deal of visual checking by teacher and fellow pupils (and, if possible, playing in front of a mirror) is necessary now, and in addition it should quickly become aurally apparent to the children that these notes

Ex.28

are among the most difficult to play in tune on the instrument.

The usual pieces necessitating the use of forward extensions follow, and it now becomes necessary to point out when extensions are essential to prepare for a note on another string. The round 'Frère Jacques' played in A major can prove a very useful exercise for this. Of the four phrases shown on page 66:

Ex. 29a involves a straightforward extension.

Ex. 29b should be played with the extended position maintained.

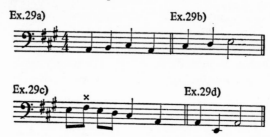

Ex. 29c is the important bar. Although a beginner might think that it would be better to play F♯ with the third finger, in fact it should be played with the second so that the hand is extended in readiness to play the C♯.

Ex. 29d can be played 1–3–1 or 1–2–1.

It is wise to go into fingering in detail like this as often as possible, since it is vital that the principles of extension fingering are understood. Frequent questions ('Which finger on the F♯ in bar six? Why?') will help to drive the point home.

The completion of this stage means that all notes normally played in first position have been covered. The group can now consolidate: D major scale, two octaves, mixing finger pattern one and forward extensions can be introduced, and A minor and D minor scales are taught, together with the arpeggios. Plenty of practice of all the notes, incorporated in pieces, scales, arpeggios, and short studies is needed. But it is equally important that the teacher should press on as fast as possible to position work.

7 Fourth Position, Half Position, Vibrato, and Harmonics

It is generally considered that of all the positions, the fourth position is the most comfortable one to teach first and this does apply particularly in group work.

(1) It is easy to find, as the angle where the neck of the instrument joins the body acts as a ready-made guide for placing the thumb.

(2) It is easy to check intonation since the first finger in this position on D, G, and C strings plays the same note as the next open string above (i.e. A, D, and G).

(3) It extends the range of notes available to top G–notes frequently needed in orchestral work.

The actual content of work suggested in this chapter may have to be altered slightly if the teacher has decided to teach fourth position before extensions in the first position, but I find that the principles do not vary, and neither does the order in which movements and notes are taught. It is merely necessary either to omit the notes which involve extensions in the fourth position, or to teach the principles of extension fingering in relation to the fourth position notes.

Remembering that difficulties, particularly in group work, still need to be introduced one at a time I divide the introductory stage into three parts:

(1) Playing the notes in the fourth position.

(2) Learning the distance to be travelled between first and fourth positions.

(3) Making the move correctly, particularly where different fingers are involved in each position.

(1) The notes are simple to find and I teach them by rote first. The pupils are asked to put the left thumb in the angle of the neck, but *not* to rest the left hand on the body of the cello on any account. The first finger is then placed on the D string so that it sounds in tune with the open A. Some teachers may prefer to ask for the first finger on the A string, but as this will sound a fifth above A the less musical pupils sometimes find it difficult to play in tune at first. Other teachers, thinking of a good hand position and bearing in mind the gap which must exist between the outside of the hand and the cello (see Plate 8), prefer to start with the first finger on the C string, which automatically ensures a good hand and elbow position. This note is, however, very difficult to hear and there is often a bad wolf note in that region, which is disconcerting for the children.

I then give a fingering drill without mentioning note names. If the group is familiar with extensions it can go like this: 1–3.4.3; 1–3.4.3; 1–2–4–2; 1–2–4–1 and I use the word 'extend' in groups three and four (1–extend–2–4–2; 1-extend-2-4-1).

This can first be played on the D string, but must ultimately be played on each string in turn. It is important to stress that the last note of the sequence, as well as the first, must be in tune with the open string above when it is played on the three lower strings. It is usually necessary to point out also that in the higher positions the bow must be used nearer the bridge.

Not until the group can play this drill with complete accuracy and confidence on all four strings do they see the notes. It is amusing, when the appropriate time comes, to produce a chart showing music with no fingering and no comment from the teacher. The leger lines on the A string are regarded with horror until the children are told that they have been playing them for weeks. Once they realize this there is usually little difficulty in persuading them to play the notes on the lower strings in fourth position too, although questions of tone colour may need to be explained.

Ex.30

It is at this stage that I find study books useful. There are one or two with several exercises using fourth position notes only (no moving involved), and giving practice on the notes on all four strings. Provided one picks short studies, or short extracts from long studies, it is easy to convince the children that they are now 'so advanced that they have graduated to studies', and they will practise them. Otherwise I find that giving studies to a group (as opposed to short exercises, which are essential and invaluable) is a waste of time, money, and the teacher's temper. Unless the studies are needed for an examination, or have a very good tune, they are not practised.

(2) Once the group is becoming familiar with the notes in fourth position the elements of changing position must be introduced. The first factor is the actual distance for the hand to move and this can be taught by the following exercise:

Ex.31

It is important to emphasize to the children that at this point fumbling will not do. The note they start from *each time* must be in tune and if the note they arrive at is not right they must think 'too sharp—I went too far', or 'too flat—I didn't go far enough', and go back and start again. Only in this way will the exact distance be registered on the brain. Any wobbling around at either end makes it impossible to get the muscular 'feel' of the move.

Difficulty can arise at this point if a pupil is still gripping the cello with the left thumb. If really cow-like sounds emerge during the move pupils should be encouraged first to 'stroke' the neck of the cello lightly with the left thumb, and then to feel that as each finger moves it 'tickles' the string and does *not* press down hard. It may be dangerous to say 'release the pressure of the finger on the string', in case that is interpreted too literally and the child takes the finger right off and hops from note to note. This can usually be checked if the notes involved in the move are played slurred, e.g.:

Ex.32

etc.

Once pupils have got the feel of the distance involved it is time to introduce the actual technique of moving. The golden rule is that one moves on the finger and string one is leaving. Like all the best rules it has its exceptions, and the most fundamental happens to be the one I teach first, namely:

Ex.33

For this move I find it better to release the lower fingers while still holding the D with the fourth finger, bunch 1, 2, and 3 together, and push the fourth finger out of the way with the first so that the impetus (with help from the left elbow) lands the hand in fourth position. The drill is given this way, in this sort of rhythm:

Ex.34

D – bunch – push – E

𝅘𝅥 – 𝅘𝅥 – 𝅘𝅥𝅮 – 𝅘𝅥

slowly at first and gradually speeding up, always emphasizing that the push leads straight to the E with no pause. The conventional type of move involved in returning from E to D, viz:

Ex.35

is taught in the following stages:

Ex.36a)   b)   c)   d)

Throughout, emphasis is on the fact that the first finger move is the distance guide and that the fourth finger bangs down on the right note and *does not* slide into place.

As these two moves embody the principles of all other moves the player will make, it is worth spending time over them. When they seem reasonably secure the teacher can proceed to the G major scale, two octaves, the upper octave of which embodies the moves outlined above:

Ex.37

When these have been well taught the scale itself usually presents few difficulties and is quickly learnt.

The way is now clear to learning further pieces and studies using fourth and first positions, the group being urged at all times to think about moving.

Meanwhile, as some of the foregoing can be rather a struggle one needs to keep working at some first position pieces which are well within the group's capabilities. There should then be no danger of losing the sense of achievement necessary for progress, which can easily be lost once the first excitement of position work wears off and the difficulties of moving become apparent.

HALF POSITION

If extensions have not been introduced to the group it will be very necessary to introduce half position now and many teachers may wish to use it before fourth position. I prefer to teach it once the principle of moving is established for a long distance, since with the very short distance involved thumbs may get 'glued' to the neck, and children may think that half position can be used without moving the hand completely. This fallacy must be avoided at all costs.

The half position is very useful and largely a matter of common sense and for this reason sometimes teachers leave it to students to work out for themselves. Once they have grasped the principles this is not difficult, but it does need to be taught and it need not take long.

Pupils are told to move their entire hand back towards

the scroll, keeping the thumb in the usual relationship to first and second finger, until the second finger is playing B on A string—in other words is resting where the first finger normally goes. Then a drill can be given such as 1.2.1.2; 4–2–4–2; 1–3–1–3; 4.3.4. 1. This involves no extensions, of course, and is easily played, although intonation needs watching. Finally the notes are introduced, and this is the most complex part of the procedure since a great many accidentals occur in this position:

Ex.38

A great deal of practice is needed to convince many children that in these two bars the first and fourth fingers are playing virtually the same note. (Purists may not agree with this, but as a beginning it is useful.) Exercises and pieces using half position can be found in various study books and tutors, and although there are not many in half position only, the movement from first to half position is so simple that it does not really matter.

The important thing is that pupils should realize that so many awkward-looking notes can be reached so easily.

VIBRATO

The question of when and how to teach vibrato is one that is almost certain to arouse furious debate at any gathering of cello teachers. I teach it as a vibration on the *sharp* side of the note *only* as soon as fourth position work is well under way, because the method I use ties up with the moving exercises. The ensuing suggestions are offered as a workable method which has proved successful many times. Presumably the stages could be adapted to any other vibrato technique.

The children are asked first to imagine that they are bouncing a ball with the left hand. This can be done away from the cello, but the essential part of the exercise is to get the feeling of 'bounce', in other words a reflex action, as the hand comes back.

When this movement is sufficiently loose the group turn their hands sideways and repeat the movement down the neck of the cello. It must be emphasized that this is *not* the usual change of position, and at the beginning it does not really matter if thumb and fingers do not touch neck and strings in the usual way. The important thing is to retain the bounce, i.e., a sudden move forward with a reflex action, and to feel that the whole arm is involved as far as the back of the shoulder. The elbow should move as well at this point, but not too much.

At first the class will probably make an even up and down stroking movement, but as soon as any members have grasped the quick bounce idea, they can be told to do a shorter bounce until the moment comes when they can anchor their thumbs anywhere they like (usually a little nearer the floor than first position) and see if they can still get the same feeling with the second finger resting on the string.

It is at this moment that difficulties really begin. Children either tighten up or produce a wobble which is uncontrolled and which sharpens and flattens the note. When either happens I make them go back to the really big bounce and then try to reproduce the 'feel' in miniature.

If they get it with the second finger they progress to the third, then the fourth, then the first. I usually use this order because second and third do seem to be the easiest for most children: the fourth tends to be weak and the first jams against the instrument at times.

This has all been done soundlessly as far as note production is concerned. One cannot keep the class together on this; each child must proceed at his own speed. On the other hand, the example of one who does any stage particularly well is always worth using.

The next stage, after the soundless fixed bounces, is the one which I call, for want of a better description, 'four moos to a bow'. This is really four separate finger vibrato movements to a bow, reproducing the feel of the previous exercises. The points to watch are:

(1)   That the note is only sharpened during the vibration and that the pad returns to its original position and does not get flatter or sharper.

(2)   That the movements at this stage are detached, controlled and even.

If problems are experienced three other dodges may be useful:

(1)   To tell the child to feel as if the skin of the finger is glued to the string, but the bone inside wants to move.

(2)   For the teacher to put a finger or hand in front of the child's finger and tell him to try to push it out of the way with short sideways jabs.

(3)   For the child to hold up his right arm, palm of hand inwards, imagine it is the cello neck, put thumb on inside and fingers on outside and get the feel of weight and bouncing this way in a slightly easier position (see Plates 9a and 9b).

When four 'moos' to a bow can be achieved fairly easily

with one finger (probably the second), the pupils must be encouraged to use each of the others in turn, gradually feeling the transfer of weight from one to another without interfering with the vibrato motion.

The next step is to increase speed without losing control—eight 'moos' to a bow. Each movement must still sound detached and the bow change must not interfere with even vibration.

Finally, the speed can be increased to twelve 'moos' and with this the pupil has very nearly achieved his vibrato.

If the group has managed to keep reasonably well together on this, I then take a very easy piece which they all know and ask them to do four vibrations to a minim, two to a crotchet and one to a quaver. It will sound pretty horrible, but even so, the open string in the example below will sound quite out of place and will give the children an idea of the ultimate aim.

Ex.39

At this point, too, the teacher should demonstrate with vibrato as much as possible.

All this may take many weeks: some children may achieve a good vibrato in a very short time, others show no sign of it. In any case, after about half a term of spending a short time at it every lesson I tend to ease off. If a child shows signs of getting a complex about not being able to do it, I tell him not to worry, but to have a go in private.

I encourage all children to use vibrato when they can, at first on long notes at the end of a piece, and then on suitable notes which occur in the middle.

In this way, sooner or later, vibrato can be taught and the result is a good firm controlled tone.

Harmonics are frequently taught before fourth position, but in group work they fit in to the scheme of things very well just after the fourth position. They are extremely useful and the octave harmonic is the one most used. The principle of getting there is similar to the change from first to fourth position 4–1 (one finger pushing another out of the way).

The octave harmonic on the cello is always played with the third finger (unlike the violin where the fourth finger is used). To find it a simple exercise of the kind given below can be taught.

Ex.40

The class is told that the third finger pushes the fourth out of the way and that in leaving the harmonic the third finger can leave the string fractionally before the fourth is banged down. (This is the only time when a 'hop', as opposed to a slide, is allowable.)

Trouble usually comes because left elbows have dropped, particularly on the A string, and the gap between the side of the left hand and the edge of the cello has not been maintained. I encourage the class to run their third fingers at harmonic pressure down the whole length of the finger-board on each string in turn, bringing the thumb out in order to reach the highest positions and allowing it to fall back into place behind the neck of the cello as the finger moves back down through the positions. The resultant sound can be fascinating and is usually greatly enjoyed, especially by the boys. The teacher will be well advised, however, to make quite sure that he can explain the scientific basis of harmonics. Alternatively a physics teacher may be pressed into service.

The work outlined in this chapter may take a considerable time. Whichever order is used, the group, although still elementary, should be able to make a really useful contribution to the school orchestra and the school concert by the time fourth position and harmonics are completed.

8 Third and Second Positions; The Tenor Clef

The contents of the previous chapter are not necessarily to be taught in the order suggested there. Half position may be taught before fourth position and fourth position before the extensions explained in Chapter 6. If, for any reason, extensions have been omitted to date the principle should really be explained and taught before proceeding to third and second position work.

Once again argument rages as to the order in which positions should be taught. I find it easier to teach fourth followed by third followed by second—firstly because the progression is logical, secondly because the third position is very easy to pitch, although the thumb has no physical guide and lastly because the third position is very comfortable to play in, whereas second can be very awkward, especially in extended position.

THIRD POSITION

The moment at which third position is tackled must depend on group and teacher. Once the principles of fingering and moving are understood, and the children are at home with notes in the fourth position, it is probably best to move on to third position as quickly as possible.

The same approach can be used as in teaching fourth position. The teacher first of all concentrates on the actual placing of the hand—first finger plays a note one octave above the next open string down and tunes from it, i.e.:

Ex.41

The group will by now be familiar with the fingering drill used for fourth position (1–3.4.3; 1–2–4.1, etc.) and are asked to play it in the new position on all strings, checking with the open strings all the time. Once the intonation is established they are shown the notes

Ex.42

The next step, to studies entirely in third position, is a short one, and the scale of F major, which involves third position, can be taught very quickly.

Ex.43

Children will want to use fourth position to play this scale, but it is as well to insist, at this stage, on the rule that every two-octave scale except C major must end on a fourth finger (or a third if it goes to the higher positions). The principles of cello scale fingering are discussed in the Appendix. F major arpeggio, on the other hand, can be played most comfortably by using fourth position:

Ex.44

Third position fingerings can quickly be incorporated into pieces and it should be possible to convince the most unwilling user of third position that this fingering is better

for passages such as those given below, even if it seems more difficult at first.

(1) **Ex.45a)**

or (2)

Ex.45b)

which uses back extension.

SECOND POSITION

Much consolidation work can be done on fourth and third positions, and the teacher must be his own judge of the time to introduce second position. As I indicated above it can be very awkward to pitch, but it does bring under the hand some very useful intervals.

One of the difficulties is teaching the placing of the hand. Most study books consider that the position is based on middle C played on the A string with the first finger, and it is probably best to work from this.

I use the same fingering drill as for fourth and third positions, asking the children to pitch their third fingers on the A string an octave above the open D. This seems to be the easiest note to hear. Great care must be exercised when the extension fingering is used that the twisted hand position, or alternatively a bad arm position, does not occur:

Ex.46

X is the dangerous group.

If there is a lot of trouble at this point it might be as well to introduce a completely different fingering drill which will encourage the pointing back of the first finger, such as:

Ex.47

In this case, of course, the *second* finger will be pitched an octave above the D string. Both drills, and many others the teacher can make up, are very useful and I would still introduce them by rote before using any notation at all.

Once again, there are studies to be found in the second position, and as much or as little time may be spent on them as required. The group will soon be able to incorporate the second position fingerings into their pieces, and use them where they occur.

Unfortunately both two-octave scales which end in second position are difficult, since they involve more than one simple move. E major is best avoided at this early stage, and even E minor, which uses half and third positions as well as second, presents considerable difficulties.

E♭ major, however, is set for a comparatively early grade of the Associated Board examinations, and as it uses both third and second positions, is a good introduction to the complexities of cello scale-fingering (dealt with briefly in the Appendix). The bottom octave will already be familiar. The upper octave may be fingered in this way:

Ex.48

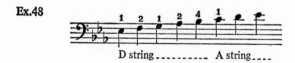

D string .... A string ....

This is the traditional fingering and teachers may wish to alter it. On the other hand it introduces a principle which can be very useful in the teaching of cello scale-fingerings.

The stage that has now been reached, with all the notes learnt up to and including the A harmonic, is one that can last a very long time. Some cellists go through life happily with very little extra, although they miss the best of the repertoire if they do stick at this point. There is a tremendous amount of material available for study and the use of fifth position (incorporating the B one whole tone higher) is easily taught as needed.

Ex.49

The thumb does not need to be moved from the neck of the instrument, and the main point to be stressed is that for elementary players, the fourth or little finger is not normally used above G. In other words the fingering principles become rather different and much closer akin to those of the violin. For example, each of the bars below will be fingered 1.2.3, with the fingers moved for the appropriate intervals:

Ex.50

etc.

TENOR CLEF

By this stage pupils should have graduated to individual lessons and group techniques should no longer be necessary.

If, however, there is a flourishing orchestra in the school it may well fall to the cello teacher to teach the tenor clef to the group at a relatively early stage. Sometimes the treble clef and the treble clef with notes needing transposition down an octave (as for tenor singers) also appear, but these should be avoided if at all possible, as they only add difficulties.

Knowledge of the tenor clef, however, is essential for every cellist and indeed the clef is used in a Grade II *Polychordia Orchestral Album*.

It is not really difficult for a cellist to learn, especially if considered in relation to the instrument from the beginning. Unfortunately there is very little material available for use with pupils. There are some good drills in the *New Way to Cello Playing Book IV*, but they are few, and more material relating the tenor clef to the bass clef in the way described below is badly needed. The teacher may well have to produce his own.

There is one simple rule: everything written in the tenor clef sounds a fifth higher than it would if written in the bass clef. As the strings are tuned in fifths, lower notes in the tenor clef can be played with the fingering for the bass clef, but one string higher. This may shock purists, but it is very practical. An example I have found useful is the one given in Ex. 51:

Ex.51

It is first played on the D string and *fingered as marked*. Then it is played on the A string with the same fingering and the group is asked the names of the notes.

Next they see it written in the tenor clef:

Ex.52

and they realize that they are simply transposing up one string. This is a method of introduction. The next step is to deal with the higher notes and it is wise to point out that the tenor clef does away with confusing leger lines.

which is easier to read at speed.

Some 'guide-posts' are useful too. The most important are E, G, and A (marked with an X above). Once these are learnt most of the other notes can be read and played by interval.

To accustom the children to changing clef quickly one can take a tune with repeated phrases and write them alternately in bass and tenor clefs—pointing out that this is only for practice.

Ex.54

This is an extreme example, and the teacher may find better ones, but drills of this sort are necessary to accustom children to the quick change of clef often required in an orchestra.

9 The Elementary Cellist in the Orchestra

Any school which encourages string teaching will either have, or be determined to build up, an orchestra. Very often this orchestra performs regularly at assembly, plays a prominent part in school concerts, accompanies shows mounted by the drama department, and is generally as important a part of school life as the football or cricket teams. Sometimes there are two orchestras and this can ease some of the difficulties which are apt to make the life of a peripatetic teacher frustrating.

The first problem which arises is to judge how soon a child is ready to enter the orchestra. A specific answer is impossible; the answer is the same as the one to that hoary old chestnut 'How long is a piece of string?'. It may well be that the cello teacher wants to keep his pupils out of the orchestra for as long as possible so that techniques can become firmly established, but it is equally certain that a keen music specialist will want the child to join in as soon as possible. In addition (see also Chapter 10) a child may be roped into general classroom music almost before he can hold a bow. So a compromise must be reached. The cello teacher can ask if his pupil may bring the parts to lessons, so that they may be edited if necessary. He can also explain to the conductor of the orchestra his pattern of work, what notes he does or does not wish pupils to play at any given time, and his standards of posture, together with the needs of cellists for special chairs and end-pin holders, as explained in Chapter 1.

I have known too many children dragged into the school orchestra early, presented with a part in an impossible key (Db major springs to mind in one case) with no attempt to 'doctor' it, and discouraged to the point of giving up within two terms. On the other hand, older and more advanced children can be equally discouraged if they are asked to play very elementary music all the time. If they can be encouraged to play the occasional easy piece very well to help the younger ones, have the bulk of the music at an intermediate level, and be stimulated to play some fairly difficult chamber music, then a reasonable solution will have been found.

The usual problems encountered in school orchestras are connected with bowing and intonation. Sometimes bowing in printed parts is bad, and if the conductor is not a string player he should be open to advice on this. An elementary player will not know the convention of up-bow for anacrusis at the beginning of a piece and certainly will not remember it. Equally he will find it impossible to bow

Ex.55

without a bump unless he runs out of bow. The techniques to deal with (d) can and should be learnt quickly and the alternative solutions to (c) taught as quickly as possible and indicated to the conductor. Sometimes it helps to bow an awkward passage so that the difficult notes come on changes of bow: this can help the intonation.

It is in the matter of playing in tune that most school orchestras fall down. Unfortunately, most violinists at an early stage prefer the keys of D and A major. A major, in particular, involves cellists in some very difficult extensions (see Chapter 6) and it should always be remembered that the notes shown in Ex. 56 are never safe, even for experienced players.

Ex.56

If approached step-wise from below there is some chance that the first three may be played in tune, but the hand often moves up the cello in the process with the result that the next first finger note will be sharp. Progressions to be avoided are:

Ex.57

(d) is particularly nasty unless it can be played in third position.

Cellists really prefer G major and C major to begin with, and can often manage F major (which is anathema to violinists at the early stages). Clarinettists, of course, always ask for B♭ major and will even push for E♭ major, which should be avoided like the plague by the strings in the early years.

Of course, this limitation on keys can be surmounted by judicious editing of parts. Very often a simple solution is to put the part up or down one octave. A classic example can be found in the opening bars of the Jig, from the Woodhouse arrangement of the *Four Pieces* from the Bach 3rd Suite in D.

Ex.58a)

As it stands it is almost impossible to play in tune in the first position. Put it up an octave and the result is perfectly acceptable and relatively simple to play.

Ex.58b)

Very often extension problems can be solved by substituting the root position instead of the third of the chord with no ill effects whatever.

e.g.

Ex.59a)

can become

Ex.59b)

and will be perfectly acceptable provided it is played musically.

It will sometimes be necessary to write a special part for a very elementary group of cellists. In this case the publisher's permission should always be sought, and will in general be given readily.

When embarking on this it must be remembered that the part must be rhythmically simple and logical, as well as containing easy notes. I have seen many so-called easy parts that were mathematically so difficult to count that no beginner could cope. This usually occurs when the key of the piece is particularly awkward (e.g. E♭ major) and the only simple notes available are F, G, C, and possibly low B♭ and E♭. But even in the key of G this sort of thing can occur:

Ex.60

Rhythmically no two bars are the same and there is no sense of rhythmic pattern. On the other hand this bass (which fits the 'Sailor's Hornpipe' in Elsie Smith's *Violin Class Book II*) has a rhythmic pattern which changes when the melody changes and is easy to teach.

Ex.61

It is designed for children playing only open strings and first finger, so that the harmony may seem a little crude. On the other hand, this disadvantage is more than outweighed at the beginning by the simplicity of the rhythmic pattern.

The problems of bowing across strings must also be borne in mind. Again, a bad bowed part for beginners may look like this:

Ex.62

Sometimes the odd slur is added as in the last bar and no indications of bowing that are helpful are given. Consideration must be given to the pupil's ability to cross strings, whether he can slur, whether he can control the speed of the bow and find the notes, and, above all, whether the bowing will work out so that down-bows (which are the accented ones) come where they are needed.

Finally there comes the actual orchestral practice itself. Too often this is a slipshod affair, nobody tunes properly, children sit badly, stands are badly placed, discipline is lax.

Everyone will enjoy themselves so much more if the following points are observed:

(1)   Suitable chairs for cellists are available (see Chapter 1).

(2)   Mats or end-pin holders are provided for the cellists so that end-pins do not slip.

(3)   Stands are placed so that each player can see the conductor over the top of the stand.

(4)   Never more than two cellists (or any other instrumentalists for that matter) are asked to share a stand.

(5)   When A-strings are being tuned *no one* in the orchestra is allowed to mess around playing other notes.

(6)   The cellists are allowed to have two or three minutes, or even more, to tune their bottom strings while everyone else is silent.

(7)   Help is given to those cellists whose hands are not strong enough to control slipping tuning pegs.

(8)   No one is allowed to talk when the conductor is speaking, let alone when anyone is playing.

In this way children will learn to listen and to play as an orchestra, part of a team, and gain a basic understanding of orchestral playing and all that it involves which will last them for the rest of their lives.

10 Incentives

There are times when learning the cello (or for that matter any stringed instrument) can only be described as a hard grind. With the changing ideas in all fields of education (and particularly the primary sector) it is essential to think of as many ways of encouraging pupils as possible. After all, the majority of them are learning in order to enjoy making music, and that enjoyment should provide them with a hobby and an interest for the rest of their lives.

Most cellists get their stimulus from playing with others. The particular problems that arise in the orchestra have been touched on in Chapter 9. However, one of the advantages of group teaching is that chamber music (or ensemble work, if one wishes to call it by a less exalted name) is possible from very early days.

The first essential is that children should learn to count while they play. Some find this very difficult, but it can be learnt, especially if it is encouraged from the very beginning. Then, even while they are still playing open strings, the children can be encouraged to accompany the teacher playing a melody on his own cello. From this they can proceed to accompanying a more advanced pupil and gradually to holding a part individually rather than as a group. There are many simple rounds within the first finger pattern which can be used to develop this independence and sometimes an ostinato can be devised for the most elementary pupils.

As an example the round 'Frère Jacques' can be played in

G major in four parts. Very elementary pupils need only
play G.D.G—either

Ex.63a)

or

Ex.63b)

—and this can be used most effectively as a pizzicato introduction, ostinato, and coda. (If elementary cellists are com-
bining with violinists who want to play this round in A
major this ostinato is even more useful since it will avoid the
problem of extensions.)

Almost any short round with simple harmonic basis can
be used like this, though it is wiser to avoid those in $\frac{6}{8}$
rhythm with ♩ ♪ patterns in them with the less experienced children. 'London's Burning', 'Hark, the Bells',
and 'Derry Ding Ding Dason' are examples of rounds
which can easily be adapted in this way. There is an increasing number of music books for classroom use now
being published which incorporate ostinati to accompany
the singing. These are worth investigating closely, but
teachers need to beware of enthusiasts who do not realize
the difficulties (particularly in using extensions) encountered by elementary cellists.

The First Year Violoncello Method book by Benoy and
Burrowes (Paxton), and *Duets and Trios* by Arthur Trew

(O.U.P.) contain many pieces with the simplest fingerings which can be used for ensemble work while the pupils are still in the earliest stages (no position work, no extensions). Once they have started position work *Twenty Trios for Young Cellists* by Benoy and Sutton (O.U.P.), the *Second Year Violoncello Method*, and later the *Third Year* . . . (Benoy and Burrowes; Paxton) are all extremely useful.

It is essential that children should be taught as early as possible to listen to each other, to blend in pitch and tone, and to start and finish without outside help—in other words, the elements of chamber music playing.

THE CELLIST IN THE CLASSROOM

Modern developments in the use of pitch percussion instruments are leading to the integration of the cellist into school music-making as a classroom activity. This is a most encouraging development, but there are two pitfalls into which an enthusiastic but unwary general music teacher may fall, which could actually discourage the child.

The first is the drone bass. While a beginner will get the greatest possible pleasure from playing an open G string for minutes at a time, a more advanced player will be bored to screaming point unless a tricky rhythm is involved. On the other hand, as pointed out in the previous chapter, an elementary player often cannot manage a tricky rhythm and gets frustrated.

The second pitfall is the use of difficult notes. Many of the so-called elementary cello parts in the new group music-making publications contain most difficult notes. It is up to the cello teacher to make contact with the class teacher, find out what is going on, and suggest some simple re-writing of parts if necessary.

ELEMENTARY CHAMBER MUSIC

This is a logical progression from either of the above. There are easy string quartets available and some easy string orchestra books such as the *Second String Band Book* by Margaretta Scott can be very useful. The *Easy for Both* series by James Brown can form the basis for a piano trio, quartet, or even quintet, and a fairly elementary cellist can join in with better players in certain movements of the Haydn Piano Trios. Compatible temperament is even more important than equality of technique for these groups to be a success. Playing chamber music is essentially an activity for friends.

EXAMINATIONS AND TESTS

The present-day trend in educational thought is moving away from examinations towards individual assessment, and the policy of the school must be taken into account when considering these. I have found that fairly informal tests, perhaps given annually, work wonders, especially if someone else knowledgeable can be brought in from outside to take them. A set piece, an 'own choice' piece, and some scales, with an aural test and a very short sight test, can be marked or graded, and the 'examiner' given if necessary some knowledge of the child's background. As a stimulus to practice in most cases these informal tests are hard to beat.

The more formal examinations organized by outside bodies, such as the Associated Board of the Royal Schools of Music or Trinity College, London, are a rather different matter. It is perfectly possible to enter an entire group for the lower grade examinations, and to get good results, but this involves a long period of work on the same music, some of which may not fit easily into the teacher's scheme of work. The culmination may well be an examination by someone who is a first-class musician, but is not a string player and does not have detailed knowledge of the early difficulties of learning a string instrument. It must be said that for many parents and children the prestige from these examinations (not least the certificate) outweighs the disadvantages, but the teacher must guard against parental pressure for the wrong reasons, and assess the pros and cons very carefully indeed.

It is important that any candidate for these examinations should have a competent accompanist who has been available for practice sessions, and who will not panic on the day.

It is ever more important that parents should not get the idea that, having passed Grade I, the child must immediately progress to Grade II, and so on through all the Grades, doing nothing else. These examinations are only a scaffolding, and much work on bricks and mortar must be done between each stage.

FESTIVALS AND CONCERTS

There are two types of festival, competitive and non-competitive, and the supporters of each generate much heat in the advocacy of the merits of the system they prefer.

The usual competitive festival consists of classes for solo players, and possibly for small groups as well. Again it must be said that the present trend of educational thought is away from competition and, therefore, the teacher will be well advised to check with the school authorities before entering pupils, especially if the festival is held during school hours. Adjudicators at these festivals are frequently excellent and although the marking is usually according to an unrealistically high convention, many children enjoy them thoroughly and it is of course possible to enter all the members of a group if a suitable piece has been set. But the teacher must beware of two very great dangers: to some sensitive children these festivals are unmitigated hell and these pupils should not be forced to enter, either by teacher or parents. (Unfortunately proud parents are too often at fault in this respect.) Secondly, the child (and the parents) must be told frequently and forcefully that the adjudication and the chance of comparing his playing with other people's are the important things, *not* the marks, and most certainly not winning the prize, cup, or certificate. This is very pleasant if it happens, but concentration on winning leads to pot-hunting, not music.

Non-competitive festivals are a very different matter. These are usually for massed forces, and the parts are learnt beforehand, rehearsed on the day, and then combined into a concert. The stimulus from these can be enormous, but the teacher owes it to the children and the festival to see that the music required is properly learnt beforehand. Otherwise frustration and disappointment can result all round.

Concerts are an incentive in which every child should be involved from a very early stage. They may be quite informal: playing for assembly at school, playing to the form, playing to a few interested people in the lunch hour (I have known a few children get up a concert themselves like this, possibly to raise money for charity). Or they may involve participation in a big formal school concert, either by playing solos, or in the orchestra, or in a small group. Whatever the nature of the concert, the fact that people are going to be listening to the child playing is a tremendous stimulus to endeavour, and well-judged applause a sweetener to the often bitter pill of practice.

In conclusion I would say that the biggest incentive of all is the feeling of progress. Well-judged praise, a reference back to something which was difficult a year ago but which is now easy, the stimulus of a constant feeling of achievement, all these carefully nurtured by the teacher, will carry the pupils forward. Group work is difficult, but when the right techniques are acquired and success is achieved, it is satisfying beyond measure.

Conclusion

In this book I have tried to set out one possible method of group teaching. There will be many teachers who will disagree with some or all of the suggestions I have made. Methods will continue to improve, new ideas will come forward, new discoveries will be made.

The important things are:

(1)   That all teaching, and group teaching above all, should follow in a logical sequence.
(2)   That all teaching should be planned.
(3)   That each lesson should be planned.
(4)   That each lesson should be enjoyed.

—and above all:

(5)   That the aim in all this is that children should grow up loving music, wanting to take part in music, and playing musically. Very few of us have the good fortune to meet a budding genius among our pupils. All of us are training amateurs and perhaps a few professionals, but the amateurs are the majority of our pupils and the parents of tomorrow, who in their turn will pass on the joy of making music.

Appendix 1

These notes are appended as a guide to any teacher who is not a cellist, but who finds himself in the unenviable position of having to advise a youngster, in an orchestra or in school, whose cello teacher is not available at the time. Non-cellists should not be teaching advanced techniques.

SCALES

Modern thinking on hand position and finger placing is revising the traditional fingering for the last three notes of the second octave of most major scales, and for harmonic scales. Because I feel that in many circumstances these fingerings must be adapted to the pupil concerned (size of hand having a great deal to do with the one chosen), I give below some rules I have found useful for traditional scale-fingerings, with a note on the most common modern departures from the rule. Those wishing to explore the matter in greater depth are referred to Maurice Eisenberg's excellent book *Cello Playing for Today* (The Strad, London).

Rule 1 was mentioned in Chapter 8 when dealing with the F major scale. This is that the top note of every two-octave major scale above middle C and of *every* two-octave minor scale be played by the fourth or third finger. (There is discussion about C harmonic minor and for this those interested should refer to p. 90 of Mr. Eisenberg's book.) *Rule 2* applies to movement between positions on the lower strings. It is this:

(a) When open strings cannot be used, start on a first finger.

(b) If possible use every finger in the position the player is in.

(c) Then move *back* one position on to a higher string, unless the note is not available. In this case move forward so that six notes are played on the first string and then move backwards after that.

Two examples may help to make this clear:

(1) E major 2 octaves:

Appendix

Ex.64

IV............ III .... II I
2nd. pos.   1st. pos.   ½pos.   3rd. pos.   2nd. pos.

(2) D♭ major 2 octaves:

Ex.65

IV .... III .... II .... I ....
½pos.   4th. pos.   3rd. pos.   2nd. pos.   ½pos.

The three moves marked (X) are all backwards one position. The exceptions to this rule are E♭ major and F major, where, in order to end on a fourth finger, the fingerings shown in Chapter 8 must be used and the lower octave can be played in first position.

In minor scales I prefer to teach a similar fingering ascending and descending, even in the melodic form, but this is a matter of preference.

Rule 3 In the third and fourth octaves of all the scales the fingering is invariably 1.2.1.2.1.2.3.

Chromatic Scales Using open strings 0.1.2.3.1.2.3.0, and on A string 1.2.3, as needed.

It is useful to try to formulate some kind of grouping for scales with related finger patterns. A rough one which I find useful for two-octave scales is as follows:

1. Scales in first and fourth positions:
    G major and minor, C minor.
2. Scale using third position only:
    F major.
3. Scales using a forward move after the first three notes:
    D♭ major, C♯ minor.
    A♭ major, G♯ minor.
4. Scales using one or more backward moves after the first three notes:
    E major, B major.
    F♯ major, and minor.
    F minor, B♭ minor.
5. Scale using third-octave fingering for second octave:
    A major.

THE THUMB POSITIONS

These should not be taught to groups, but, if the need arises, non-cellists in particular should look for the following:

(1) The thumb should be placed square across two strings, holding both down.

(2) The hand should be square.

(3) The thumb should be one whole tone behind the first finger.

Three useful aids to thumb-position work are:

(1) Encourage the pupil to bring the thumb out and place it on the strings behind the other fingers while they are still holding notes in fourth position.

(2) Teaching a thumb position scale, e.g.:

Ex.66

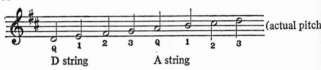

N.B. As far as the placing of first, second, and third fingers are concerned 'violin-type' principles of finger placing are now the rule.

(3) Teaching the move into thumb position:

Ex.67

X: this note should be eliminated, but the feel of the move must be established, and it is preferable to bring the thumb above the string while the fingers are still holding down F and G.

If you are not a cellist and have never done this work, remember that the thumb gets very sore and do *not* go on too long!

Appendix II

No attempt is being made in this book to give an exhaustive list of teaching material. Any such list goes out of date very quickly and in any case the *Graded List of String Class Teaching Music,* together with the Supplements, published by the Rural Music Schools Association, Little Benslow Hills, Hitchin, Herts, describes fully music which has actually been used in group work and recommended by experienced teachers. Full details of all the music mentioned in the text will be found in these lists.

I have found, however, that it is useful to keep by me a list of melodies with simple rhythms that can be played in one finger pattern only and which can be transposed into various keys to meet the needs of each finger pattern. There are many of these, but I have found all of the following useful:

MELODIES OF 6 NOTES OR LESS
Suo-Gân
Do, do, l'enfant do
Pease pudding hot
Go from my window
Go and tell Aunt Nancy
J'ai du bon tabac
Twinkle, twinkle little star
The deaf old woman's courtship

RANGE OF AN OCTAVE
  Cock-a-doodle-doo
  Roman Soldiers (old English singing game)
  Vilikins and his Dinah
  The old woman and the pedlar
  Upon Paul's steeple

RANGE A LITTLE MORE THAN AN OCTAVE
  The Vicar of Bray
  Turn the glasses over

HYMNS
  Tallis's ordinal
  Nicaea (Holy, holy, holy)
  Franconia (Blest are the pure in heart)
  Monkland (Let us with a gladsome mind)
  Duke Street (Fight the good fight)
  St. Theodulph (All glory, laud, and honour)
  Eudoxia (Now the day is over)
  Easter Alleluia

CAROLS
  Unto us a boy is born
  The first Nowell
  A child this day is born
  Past 3 o'clock (chorus only)
  From out of a wood did a cuckoo fly

ROUNDS
  Frère Jacques
  London's Burning
  Derry ding ding dason
  Turn again, Whittington
  Kookaburra